**Rotten Boroughs, Political Thickets,
and Legislative Donnybrooks**

Number Thirty-seven
Jack and Doris Smothers Series
in Texas History, Life, and Culture

Rotten Boroughs, Political Thickets, and Legislative Donnybrooks

Redistricting in Texas

EDITED BY GARY A. KEITH

University of Texas Press ⬥ *Austin*

Publication of this work was made possible in part by support from the J. E. Smothers, Sr., Memorial Foundation and the National Endowment for the Humanities.

Requests for permission to reproduce material from this work should be sent to:
Permissions
University of Texas Press
P.O. Box 7819
Austin, TX 78713-7819
http://utpress.utexas.edu/about/book-permissions

♾ The paper used in this book meets the minimum requirements of ANSI/NISO Z39.48-1992 (R1997) (Permanence of Paper).

Library of Congress Cataloging-in-Publication Data
Rotten boroughs, political thickets, and legislative donnybrooks : redistricting in Texas / edited by Gary A. Keith. — First edition.
    pages   cm. — (Jack and Doris Smothers series in Texas history, life, and culture ; number thirty-seven)
    Includes bibliographical references and index.
    ISBN 978-0-292-74540-7 (cl. : alk. paper)
    1. Apportionment (Election law) — Texas.   2. Election districts — Texas.
    3. Demography — Political aspects — Texas.   4. Texas — Politics and government.   I. Keith, Gary.
    JK4868.R67   2013
    328.764′07345 — dc23   2013001171

doi:10.7560/745407

This book is dedicated to the memory of Thomas Paine, who wrote that "The true and only true basis of representative government is equality of rights. Every man has a right to one vote, and no more, in the choice of representatives."

Contents

Preface

Legislative redistricting brawls are the quintessential American game of politics. But more than a game, redistricting creates profound and long-lasting effects by shifting the fortunes of political parties, individual politicians, and racial, ethnic, and community representation, thus potentially redirecting policy outcomes. In this volume, we seven political scientists and lawyers seek to shine a spotlight on the world of Texas congressional, state legislative, and local redistricting. Those redistricting outcomes have not just affected Texas politics; national leaders have emerged from and engaged in Texas redistricting battles. The 2003 Texas redistricting shenanigans entertained the nation as Democratic legislators fled, first to Oklahoma, then to New Mexico, in unsuccessful attempts to thwart redistricting plans that hurt them. In 2011, for the first time since the 1870s, Republicans controlled the Texas House, Texas Senate, and governorship during a regular redistricting session and consolidated their status, much as partisan majorities state after state, decade after decade, have done. In this volume, we seek to provide historical, institutional, legal, legislative, realpolitik, and sociological insight into the history of redistricting in Texas.

Acknowledgments

I wish to thank those who graced the halls of the Texas capitol during those years that I worked at the legislature and learned legislative politics, especially Tom Whatley and my former colleagues at the House Study Group, House Research Organization, and Legislative Study Group. I would also like to thank Travis County Commissioner Sarah Eckhardt and my former Texas Department of Agriculture colleague Pete McRae, who spurred me to take up the topic of Texas redistricting. I thank the community at the University of the Incarnate Word for the support I have gotten there these past five years. Finally, I thank my fellow contributors to this volume — José Garza, Seth C. McKee, Mark J. McKenzie, J. D. Pauerstein, David R. Richards, and Craig A. Washington — for volunteering their skills, knowledge, and insights on Texas redistricting.

Acronyms

AVAP	Anglo Voting Age Population
BVAP	Black Voting Age Population
DOJ	U.S. Department of Justice
GIS	Geographic Information Systems
GOP	Grand Old Party [Republican Party]
HVAP	Hispanic Voting Age Population
ISD	Independent School District
LRB	Legislative Redistricting Board
LULAC	League of United Latin American Citizens
MALDEF	Mexican American Legal Defense and Educational Fund
NAACP	National Association for the Advancement of Colored People
OVAP	Others Voting Age Population
SVREP	Southwest Voter Registration Education Project
TAB	Texas Association of Business
TLC	Texas Legislative Council
TRLA	Texas Rural Legal Aid/Texas RioGrande Legal Aid
TRMPAC	Texans for a Republican Majority
TSU	Texas Southern University
VAP	Voting Age Population
VRA	U.S. Voting Rights Act
VTD	Voting Tabulation District

Prologue: Scope and Methods

This work is a tapestry. Redistricting analyses typically adopt a specific methodological approach, or topical focus, or address a particular time period or institution. We do not quarrel with any of those approaches—indeed, several of us use such approaches in our own work. In this volume, though, we seek to weave together an understanding of Texas redistricting through the voices and analyses of political scientists, lawyers, and practitioners. We believe that by presenting viewpoints and approaches from these differing vantage points, readers will gain a clearer, richer, and more complete understanding of redistricting realities than is possible through just one approach.

Political scientists seek to assemble redistricting data, test hypotheses, and fashion theories to build an understanding of redistricting; lawyers seek to use precedent to defend a policy in court, or, using unique fact situations from a redistricting outcome, break new legal ground with innovative legal theories; practitioners seek to protect an existing power bloc or to increase representation from groups that they perceive to be underrepresented in the legislative process.

This volume is unique in that we ask lawyers, social scientists, legislators, and general readers to explore one another's approaches and seek commonalities. Social scientists who look for data-rich analysis and hypothesis testing will find that in Chapter 6; lawyer-litigators who follow case history and doctrine development will find them in several chapters; citizens and general readers will see good examples of these varying approaches and, we hope, learn the value of each. Every chapter is different, then, by design. We approach fifty years of Texas redistricting from all these perspectives, with the intent that, by the end, the explorations, data analyses, histories, and observations will build a realpolitik understanding of redistricting, revealing who benefits from it and why.

In the introduction, "The Prequel—Unequal Representation," Gary A. Keith provides a brief review of recent literature on redistricting, succinctly describes the twentieth-century history of Texas redistricting, and lays out the critical U.S. Supreme Court cases that altered the redistricting landscape. That history begins with the Texas legislature shirking its duty to redistrict in order to protect the governing rural (and white) bloc. Even when the legislature began redistricting again mid-century, it produced state legislative and congressional districts with significant population variances—with rural areas overrepresented and urban (and minority) areas underrepresented. The U.S. Supreme Court decisions of the early 1960s changed the power dynamics by declaring that redistricting outcomes were justiciable issues, as they involved compliance first with the Equal Protection Clause of the Constitution, then with the Voting Rights Act (VRA). The Texas legislature was compelled not only to redistrict, but to meet standards the judiciary determined were essential to achieve equal representation.

In Chapter 1, "Entering the Thicket: 1965," Keith revisits Texas's 1965 redistricting, the first done after *Baker v. Carr* and other court decisions forced Texas to embed political equality in its decennial carvings. That 1965 battle was triangulated between the dominant conservative Democratic faction, the weaker liberal/labor/minority Democratic faction, and the emerging Republican Party. The redistricting both foreshadowed and shaped modern Texas politics, including a shift to urban dominance, racial/ethnic politics, partisan battles, and ideological conflicts.

In Chapter 2, "Legislating in the Thicket," Craig A. Washington introduces us to legislative and congressional politics—the kitchens of redistricting. In the kitchen of the Texas legislature, Speaker politics, policy battles, Anglo-Black-Hispanic dynamics, party politics, and high office ambitions are all aswirl every session—and redistricting is just another seasoning added as the sausage ingredients are ground and mixed once a decade. Washington's choice to throw in with the winning Speaker candidate in 1975 led to his inside seat with the leadership team during the 1981 redistricting. His leadership on behalf of the Black Caucus, the Houston legislators, the Speaker's interests, and Democrats in general shows the complexity of the internal politics affecting redistricting. Then, in the 1991 session, Washington was a congressman, returning to the state legislature at the behest of the Texas Democratic delegation in Washington, D.C., to lobby for the seats of Democratic incumbents. Craig Washington is also an attorney, and he describes his experiences combining litigation strategizing along with his legislator roles.

In Chapter 3, "Litigating Texas Redistricting: A Democratic Lawyer's Experience," David R. Richards explains the time line of Texas redistricting litigation from the 1970s to the early twenty-first century. Richards was an attorney for plaintiffs in many of those cases. In the 1980s, he represented the Texas attorney general, defending the state's redistricting plans. Richards describes the legal strategies and courtroom dramatics that he and other litigators engaged in, portraying the back-and-forth litigation, in state and federal courts, as a continuous chess match. Lawyers represent their clients; Richards often sued the State of Texas on behalf of his clients (Democratic and minority legislators, candidates, and constituents); yet when he went inside with the new attorney general, he switched sides and defended the State. Lawyers have considerable leeway, though, in steering litigation for policy objectives, and Richards's ends were often the same whether he was inside or outside.

In Chapter 4, "Texas Redistricting: A Republican Lawyer's Perspective," J. D. Pauerstein begins with the battles that Republicans fought against the majority Democrats in the 1980s legislatures, then plunges into the fiercely contested battles of the 1990s, when Republicans became ascendant. If redistricting is a game of the powerful protecting their power, then in the context of the century-long dominance of Texas politics by Democrats, the Republicans were constantly fighting an uphill battle for representation in the legislature. When they lost there (as they usually did), the courtroom became the next battleground. As Republican statewide candidates began winning (especially the governorship), Republican litigators had a power chip they lacked in earlier battles. The combination of inroads to political power in the state, coupled with national political developments, allowed Pauerstein and others in the Republican legal team to joust with Richards and the Democrats' legal team and win victories that they had not won before.

Redistricting is not solely a state-level matter. In Chapter 5, "The Voting Rights Organizers," José Garza describes local grassroots efforts in Texas that reached up to the courts and expanded voting rights. Local governments, too, must redistrict—and because there are so many local governments, much of the redistricting skirmishes happen locally, even if they do not get the popular attention that state legislative and congressional redistricting get. The concepts that were established in the legislative and congressional litigation cases cascaded down into local government voting equality cases in Texas as well. Garza and other lawyers from advocacy groups were swamped with pleas from local communities to help. Garza describes the application of the court precedents to local governance, the resistance from local governments, and the criticality of organizing and persistence from local residents, coupled with skilled legal counsel.

In Chapter 6, "Analyzing Redistricting Outcomes," Seth C. McKee and Mark J. McKenzie use descriptive and multivariate analyses to examine the partisan and incumbent protection dynamics in Texas redistricting in the 1990s and to show how redistricting affected the parties and incumbents from 2002 to 2010. McKee and McKenzie examine the levels of support constituents grant each party and its respective incumbents before and after redistricting, versus how much support constituents grant a different incumbent following redistricting. They put the recent and current redistricting dynamics into the broader picture of long-term class-and-race political economy structure and power battles in Texas. With modern, sophisticated computerization of voting data, legislators are able to use redistricting to pick their constituents, rather than the other way around. McKee and McKenzie describe how legislators use redistricting to disrupt (or maintain) the electoral relationship between incumbents and their longtime constituents.

Finally, in the conclusion, "Redistricting Redux: 2011 and Beyond," and the epilogue, Keith broadly outlines the ongoing efforts to redistrict Texas lines after the 2010 census. The dynamics described and explained in the first six chapters are revisited, demonstrating their continuity. Lessons learned from Chapters 1 through 6 provide a ten-point rubric for analysts, citizens, legislators, and lawyers to use in coming to a more focused understanding of this decade's Texas redistricting.

**Rotten Boroughs, Political Thickets,
and Legislative Donnybrooks**

The Prequel: Unequal Representation

GARY A. KEITH

When the 2010 census numbers became available, Texas and the other 49 states plunged into the 2011 legislative and congressional redistricting season, then immediately segued into defending their legislative work in numerous court challenges. These current dynamics did not begin tabula rasa, but rather grew out of a century of political, legal, and constitutional skirmishes that built the framework for modern redistricting. We can better understand the politics and outcomes of these contemporary battles through examining the legal and political history of earlier Texas battles, including their critical players, litigation strategies and outcomes, and political power resources.

The twentieth century began with Texas and other states simply (illegally) refusing to redraw state legislative and congressional district lines. The fundamental reason was that resisting redistricting provided more benefits to those wielding power than complying with constitutional and legal commands to act. Judicial action mid-century reversed the incentive/disincentive equation; the Texas legislature reluctantly, begrudgingly resumed its redistricting role in the 1950s and 1960s. Then, by the late twentieth century, politics became more nationalized, party discipline (through campaign finance rewards) grew stronger, party unity rose, judicial mandates became murkier, and the need for and benefits of redistricting were more immediate. Thus, the 2011 redistricting occurred against the historical backdrop of the 1965 effort, the subsequent court-scrutinized puzzle making, congressional passage and application of the Voting Rights Act, and the currents of modern power struggles.

Political scientists intensely scrutinize redistricting dynamics and outcomes, and the scrutiny heightens with the turning of the decennial clock. Since the 2001 round of redistricting, Nathaniel Persily has reviewed the debates over rules versus standards, group rights versus individual rights, activism versus restraint, and the consequences of the judicial revolution, including increased urban representation. He concludes that there do not appear to be systemic partisan effects to the redistrictings.[1] Winburn has described the 2001 redistricting train wreck in Texas, arguing that the "partisan commission" that is the Texas Legislative Redistricting Board had long pursued the primary goal of incumbent (conservative Democrat) protection, then switched to the goal of partisan (Republican) advance. He notes that "partisan commissions represent the wild card of the theoretical typologies of redistricting control. By design, partisan commissions take away the direct power of redistricting away [*sic*] from the legislature, but keep the partisanship."[2]

In preparation for the 2011 round of redistricting, the National Conference of State Legislatures reviewed the legal and political landscape, including the 2006 Texas case *LULAC v. Perry*, in which the Court rejected the argument that the partisan gerrymander in the existing plan was cause for judicial concern.[3] Hebert et al. have also noted the partisan gerrymander issue, but then concentrated on Voting Rights Act issues as the central focus of 2011 redistricting.[4] Perales, Figueroa, and Rivas have produced a thorough review of voting discrimination policies in Texas, including state and local redistricting issues, with a focus on Voting Rights Act litigation.[5] Finally, in a series of articles, Seth C. McKee (contributor to this volume) and various coauthors have framed recent Texas redistricting dynamics within the context of the rise of southern Republicans and have examined the question of the dropoff of voter participation when redistricting results in nonincumbents being on the ballot.[6]

The six chapters in this volume view Texas redistricting dynamics from six different perspectives. The era under examination begins with modern redistricting in 1965 and culminates with current dynamics. Before the contributors explore that period, let us briefly examine how we reached the current state of affairs with Texas redistricting.

There's Something Rotten in Texas

Like England of old, for many decades Texas—and other states[7]—cultivated "rotten boroughs": legislative districts that were grossly unequal in population and thus produced misrepresentation in the halls of government. Some legislators—and thus some citizens—were quite literally more equal than others, from the late nineteenth century to well past the mid-twentieth century. The reasons for this unequal representation include demographic changes, economic conditions, and (of course) exercises of raw political power. As farmers were driven off their land due to depressed economic conditions and the concentration of land ownership, they moved to cities, leaving fewer and fewer people in the countryside. Thus, when the constitutionally mandated decennial U.S. Census triggered redistricting for the Texas state legislature and Congress, the dominant rural legislators found that they no longer had the population base from which to sustain their power. Chumlea and Claunch have each explored how the legislature refused to redistrict when it was required to in the regular sessions of 1901, 1911, and 1921, reluctantly doing so in special sessions only with pressure from the governors.[8]

A convenient tool for incumbent (and rural) protection was simply to add more seats to the Texas House of Representatives, which legislators did each decade. In 1921, though, the House size reached its constitutional cap at 150 seats. So, in 1931, rather than draw districts reflecting the population shift to cities, legislators refused to act at all, thus keeping the 1921 districts in place. Another stonewalling came a decade later, so that over time the districts became less and less equal, rural representation in the legislature and Congress was magnified far beyond its base, and urban representation was stymied. The population shift was inexorable—so, in 1936, legislators boldly pushed through a constitutional amendment to cap urban representation at its low level, to ensure that rural representation would permanently dominate. In 1931, *The Dallas Morning News* quoted a legislator making the argument that cities were "breeding places for bolshevism, anarchy and crime waves"; another legislator stated: "I am opposed to concentrating the legislative representation in the larger cities. . . . Five members is sufficient for any one county."[9]

With self-interested rural representatives protecting their seats, and with a state constitutional victory squelching urban representation, the legislature produced the rotten boroughs of malapportionment (unequal representation). In the 1930s, the smallest Texas House district was 52 percent under the ideal (equal population) size, while the largest was 158 percent of the ideal.[10] Since the legislature refused to redistrict again in 1941, but instead kept the 1921 districts, the inequalities deepened. The gap in the 1940s was 55 percent under to 210 percent over the ideal.[11] The continuing malapportionment was protected by the Texas constitution, by the skewed political power in the legislature, by illegal voting schemes that kept the electorate virtually all white, and by the U.S. Supreme Court's doctrine that such matters were "political questions" untouchable by the judiciary. But the increasing urban (and south Texas) populations demanded better representation. They kept up the pressure and finally won enough support in Austin until, in 1947, legislators reluctantly agreed to a constitutional change that would control the decisions of future legislatures: a new Legislative Redistricting Board would be created (beginning in 1953) and empowered to act if the legislature ever again refused to redistrict itself.[12] Note that this did not affect congressional redistricting, nor did it compel equality—just passage of the bills. Rather than cede such a crucial political task as redistricting to a board dominated by higher-office politicians,[13] the legislature finally redistricted itself in 1951. Yet, with the constitutional grandfathering of low urban representation, the malapportionment continued.

By the 1950s, Texas's population was 63 percent urban. The

largest and most urban area of the state—Harris County (Houston)—elected eight state representatives in 1950 when, if not for the constitutional ceiling, it should have had fifteen. Combined, the state's most urban areas—Houston, Dallas, Fort Worth, and San Antonio—held 29 percent of the state's population, but the 1936 constitutional amendment capped their representation at 19 percent in the House and 13 percent in the Senate. When urban interests finally won additional seats with a 1951 redistricting vote, the rural House members immediately regrouped and attacked with a vote to take away the newly gained urban representation. After some arm-twisting, the measure barely got the required 100 votes (101–25), but it was not taken up in the Senate.[14] Moreover, the legislature preferred multimember, at-large (typically countywide or multicounty) districts rather than single-member districts that could allow labor or racial and ethnic minorities— or Republicans—to win.[15] In the final results of the redistricting for the 1950s, the smallest House district was 43 percent of the ideal size; the largest was 196 percent of the ideal.[16]

As for congressional representation, with the 1950 census, the state gained one congressional seat; yet, as it often did to avoid the pain of redistricting, the legislature chose to keep the old lines and make that new seat an at-large, statewide seat. Thus, the population range in the districts varied from 216,371 at the low (rural) end to 951,527 in a Dallas district.[17] Finally, in time for the 1958 election, the legislature redrew congressional districts, creating a second seat in Harris County (won by conservative Democratic County Judge Bob Casey) to go with Democratic Congressman Albert Thomas's seat.

Soon after, the 1960 census triggered the next decennial round of redistricting, for both the legislature and Congress. Burgeoning urban populations and the antiestablishment election in 1958 had produced even more pressure, and the new districts did a better job in effecting equal representation. But better didn't mean one-to-one equality[18]—it simply meant that the smallest district was 47 percent under the ideal, while the largest was only 66 percent over the ideal, rather than the 210 and 196 percentages of earlier redistrictings.[19] Moreover, the maintenance of multimember districts, coupled with the reality of race-based voting, made it nearly impossible for a minority to win a legislative seat. For instance, in 1962 Barbara Jordan lost her race for a seat in the state House of Representatives, and she lost again in 1964, 78,000–62,000.

In the 1960 census, Texas had 9,579,677 residents. With reapportionment, Texas gained yet another congressional seat. Its 23 congressional districts, then, should each have contained 416,508 residents. Once again, the legislature could not agree on congressional redistricting and made the new seat at-large. The new districts were still skewed from equal sizes—Bruce Alger's Republican Dallas district (939,845 residents) was more than twice the size of the ideal, while Democrat Wright Patman's rural east Texas district was 44 percent under the average. Ray Roberts's rural district (213,374 residents) was the farthest under the ideal. In San Antonio, Henry B. González's district had 682,481 residents. In Houston, Albert Thomas and Bob Casey each represented just over 618,000 residents.[20] Harris County was 410,000 residents over the ideal population for two seats—almost exactly the required number for an entire additional seat. And, creating long-lasting resentment, the new plan also cost Republicans the only two congressional seats they held at the time.[21]

Abandoning the Metaphor of the Political Thicket: Elevating Redistricting to a Constitutional Question of Equality

For much of the nation's history, the judiciary has been determined to not engage in authoritative actions to broaden voting rights.[22] The classic U.S. Supreme Court case that squelched judicial presence in legislative redistricting was *Colegrove v. Green* (1946).[23] Justice Felix Frankfurter straightforwardly reaffirmed the Court's long-held position that the judiciary should not and could not accept cases challenging reapportionment and redistricting. The Court, he wrote, "has refused to do so because due regard for the effective working of our Government revealed this issue to be of a peculiarly political nature, and therefore not meet for judicial determination." His oft-quoted assertion from the case is that "Courts ought not to enter this political thicket." So where to? "The remedy for unfairness in districting is to secure state legislatures that will apportion properly, or to invoke the ample powers of Congress," Frankfurter wrote. Thus spoke the Court—but it was a divided Court, and despite Frankfurter's wishes, did not settle the issue.

By the 1960s, malapportionment had become more egregious across the nation—or perhaps simply more embarrassing in the civil rights era; Tennessee's representation ratio was 44-1 and California's was 449-1.[24] By 1962, there was also a new Court, and in *Baker v. Carr*,[25] it ruled for the first time that state legislative reapportionments are justiciable issues. In one sense, Frankfurter has been proven correct: *Baker* has thrown the states, Congress, and numerous interest groups into the thicket, where they've clawed and scratched and bled since then. If, since 1962, questions about number and size and configuration of legislative seats are justiciable, then the pertinent questions are copious, and the cases throwing those questions at the courts poured forth immediately from many states.[26] In *Gray v. Sanders* (1963),[27] the Court ruled that representation by unit systems rather than human population is unconstitutional. Justice William O. Douglas wrote that the concept of political equality in our constitutional documents means "one person, one vote." In a 1964 Georgia case, *Wesberry v. Sanders*,[28] the Court specifically held that the one person, one vote standard applied to malapportioned congressional districts and referenced the historical rotten boroughs that the Constitution prohibits. Justice Hugo Black wrote, "We do not believe that the Framers of the Constitution intended to permit . . . vote-diluting discrimination to be accomplished through the device of districts containing widely varied numbers of inhabitants." Black hearkened to the constitutional convention debate over the Connecticut Compromise. "The delegates were quite aware of what Madison called the 'vicious representation' in Great Britain whereby 'rotten boroughs' with few inhabitants were represented in Parliament on or almost on a par with cities. . . . The delegates referred to rotten borough apportionments in some of the state legislatures as the kind of objectionable governmental action that the Constitution should not tolerate in the election of congressional representatives."

In the same year as *Wesberry*, the Court ruled in *Reynolds v. Sims*[29] that the one person, one vote standard applied to state legislative districts—even state senates. "Legislators represent people, not trees or acres," Chief Justice Earl Warren wrote. "We hold that, as a basic constitutional standard, the Equal Protection Clause requires that the seats in both houses of a bicameral state legislature must be apportioned on a population basis." States' rights advocates pushed measures in Congress to strip courts of jurisdiction over redistricting issues and, though they came close, ultimately did not win passage of their measures.[30] Thus, the sequence of 1962–1964 cases—*Baker, Gray, Wesberry, Reynolds*—set the stage for legislative, political, and legal redistricting actions in Texas in 1965 and after. We begin our analysis with this judicial opening of the thicket.

Political scientist E. E. Schattschneider theorized that the dominant powers in a conflict seek to contain the conflict (keep it limited to the battling parties) because they already have the upper hand—whereas the weaker parties seek to socialize the conflict (i.e., open it to new parties), creating chaos, upending the given balance of power, and producing the possibility of knocking off the dominant power. Schattschneider wrote, "We are bound to suppose therefore that control of the scale of conflict has always been a prime instrument of political strategy, whatever the language of politics may have been."[31] Schattschneider's thesis—published just two years before the *Baker* decision—could also well have suggested "whatever the language of law may have been." Frankfurter's political thicket (besides other rationales it may have had) privatized the redistricting conflict and benefited the incumbent powers. The six perspectives in this volume demonstrate that the Warren Court set off an earthquake in the thicket, and that in the ensuing socialized conflict, the balance of power was shaken.

Yet we cannot understand current dynamics merely by acknowledging that period of upheaval. Rather, over time, the conflicting parties seek new tools, new fields, and new allies to rebalance the power in their favor. Legal rulings—be they the 1960s rulings of the Warren Court or the 1990s rulings of the Rehnquist Court—are themselves outcomes of political power plays. The Texas redistrictings from 1965 to 2011 can best be understood as dynamic struggles for power—and the six perspectives in this book seek to bring together data, history, personality, court rulings, legislative politics, partisan and ideological alignments, and citizen participation to produce a more robust—and realpolitik—picture of the journey from rotten boroughs to equalized districts to partisan and demographic gerrymandering in Texas. Using these redistricting experiences and the current ongoing redistricting drama, we will conclude by applying the lessons learned from our 40-year wilderness trek to highlight the emerging pattern with ten redistricting rules.

CHAPTER 1

Entering the Thicket: 1965

GARY A. KEITH

The early 1960s Supreme Court cases, especially *Baker*, *Gray*, *Wesberry*, and *Reynolds*, set the stage for Texas congressional and state legislative redistrictings in 1965. The unequal districts established in 1961, the at-large congressional seat, and the cases brewing in Washington were burrs under the legislative saddle. In 1963, the legislature passed another congressional redistricting bill, but could not come to agreement in conference, so the bill died. In a special session, the legislature revamped the state legislative seats, lessening the underrepresentation of urban areas in the House but increasing them in the Senate.

Governor John Connally was particularly vexed by the *Reynolds* ruling that state senates must be based on population. He blasted the justices for being politically motivated. Harris County's Democratic State Representative Bob Eckhardt supported *Reynolds* and opposed Connally: "The court is entitled to its constitutional function and was not acting politically," he argued.[1] Harris County Republican party leader George H. W. Bush also chimed in, criticizing Connally for injecting "political name-calling into a matter which on its merits transcends party politics."[2] Connally recommended that the Texas legislature support a U.S. constitutional amendment to sustain the capability of states to elect senates by counties or other units. "I feel very strongly that the very essence of representative government is damaged if this proposal fails," he warned.[3] The legislature obliged by passing a resolution calling for an amendment to the U.S. Constitution to overturn *Reynolds*.[4]

Clearly, if significant changes were to come about effecting equal representation, they were not likely to be bred in the state capitol. West Texas oil businessman George H. W. Bush had moved to Houston (Harris County) and in the early sixties was serving as the county Republican chair.[5] Bush and other Republicans argued that Republicans had been repeatedly gerrymandered out of legislative and congressional seats that rightly should have been theirs, given the increase in Republican voting. On the other side of the partisan divide, the "wave" election of 1958 had brought a handful of Houstonians to the state legislature from the labor/liberal wing of the Democratic Party, including Bill Kilgarlin and Bob Eckhardt. Kilgarlin lost his seat in 1960, but was elected chair of the county's Democratic Party. Kilgarlin and a coalition of state legislators argued that equal-sized districts and single-member districts were essential.

Out of the Harris County milieu came two lawsuits from the county party chairs. In 1963 George Bush became the lead litigant in a suit challenging the constitutionality of the state's congressional districts (*Bush v. Martin*), with William (Bill) Cassin as their attorney. William (Bill) Kilgarlin became the lead litigant with Representatives Eckhardt and Jake Johnson and Senators Franklin Spears and Don Kennard in a lawsuit challenging the state legislative districts (*Kilgarlin v. Martin*), with former Representative Tony Korioth as their lawyer.[6]

In October 1963 a Special Federal Court in Houston ruled in *Bush v. Martin* declaring Texas's congressional apportionment unconstitutional. The three-judge court wrote that the overrepresentation and underrepresentation throughout the state was "spectacular" and that redistricting across the entire state was necessary to remedy the situation. The U.S. Supreme Court upheld that decision in March 1964. The district court then stayed its order until January 11, 1965, so that the 1964 elections proceeded under the old districts. If the 1965 legislature were to fail to act, the court declared, all Texas congressmen would have to run statewide. Governor Connally, Lieutenant Governor

Preston Smith, and Speaker Byron Tunnell ordered the Legislative Council to study congressional redistricting issues leading up to the 1965 session.

Meanwhile, Kilgarlin had filed his lawsuit against the state legislative districts. As the 1965 session was about to begin, a three-judge federal court (and the subsequent appellate court in 1966) invalidated four elements of those districts: (1) the requirement that only "qualified electors" be represented, (2) the provision that no county could have more than seven Texas House members, (3) a scheme for state legislative "flotorial" districts,[7] and (4) the Texas constitutional and statutory provisions that prevented any county from having more than one member in the Texas Senate.

1965: The Texas Legislature Redistricts Under Court Order

When the 1965 session began, John Connally was governor, Preston Smith was lieutenant governor and Senate president, and across the rotunda, young Ben Barnes was the new House Speaker. Barnes appointed Gus Mutscher to chair the redistricting committee.

Clearly, Harris County, as the largest county, was the critical puzzle piece in any redistricting plan. Redistricting dynamics were stirring just as Houston's longtime Congressman Albert Thomas was experiencing serious health problems and State Representative Eckhardt was testing the waters for a run for his seat.[8] The Legislative Council's redistricting study committee recommended increasing Harris County's congressional districts from two to three—and proposed lines creating a northern Harris County district, a second that was a belt across the middle of the county, and a southern district.[9] Eckhardt visited Houston businessmen to argue that since there would likely be three districts, they should support protection of the new conservative Congressman Casey and his Democratic district, a new Republican district, and a liberal-labor district, so that each camp had a voice in representing Houston.

The Legislative Council's plan, seen as the legislative leadership's plan, came to be known as "Plan A." The Council also proposed a "Plan B" pitting six incumbents in races against one another in an apparent effort to create incentives for incumbents to support Plan A. Indeed, Congressman Casey endorsed Plan A. Eckhardt, though, opposed Plan A and introduced his own plan, one supported by Bush and the Harris County Republicans.[10] His alternative came to be called the "Eckhardt/Republican" Plan.

Eckhardt and Bush proposed a pie-shaped configuration of three congressional districts, carving out an east/northeast Harris County congressional district (Thomas's District 8) from the labor-dominated communities, a new western Houston district for Bush, and a central/southern county seat (Casey's District 22). Eckhardt's and Bush's aims were similar—a Republican district, a Democratic district dominated by business-establishment conservatives, and a district that might be won by either liberal/labor or establishment Democrats.

Chairman Mutscher introduced HB 67 (Congress), HB 195 (Texas House), and SB 547 (Senate), bills that (after amendments) eventually became laws. Eckhardt filed HB 42 as his congressional redistricting proposal as well as HB 654, proposing single-member state legislative districts. Mutscher's bills proposed a Houston congressional district system similar to the interim study committee's plan: east-west tiered districts. The Legislative Council's analysis of Mutscher's bills argued that "conservative Democrats can nominate both Congressional and Legislative candidates in the Primaries, in the CENTRAL and SOUTH Districts," conceding that the northern district might go liberal. As for racial issues, their analysis made the disingenuous statement (ignoring the concept of "cracking"—dividing a population into numerous districts so that they were not a majority in any one district): "Negro population divided between three districts—no discrimination."[11] For Houston's state legislative districts, the Legislative Council concluded: "Conservative candidates can be nominated in the primary but must have the liberal/loyal Democrats to win in November."[12] Eckhardt denounced the leadership's plan as "schizophrenic." He said that "the principle should be to keep people of the same viewpoint together in order to keep the maximum number of people satisfied with their congressman."[13] Bill Cassin, the GOP attorney, sided with Eckhardt on the pie-shaped plan. Eckhardt described Plan A as a horizontal tornado "sucking the voting power out of Baytown [in the east]" and Cassin and Eckhardt said it would rob west Houston Republicans of a congressman.

Eckhardt argued that the pie-shaped pattern would allow for future redistricting in that lines could be moved to accommodate population shifts.[14] He also tried to get Mutscher and his committee to support single-member districts.[15] There was ample technical analysis to support single-member state legislative districts,[16] but the leadership did not support it. Eckhardt worked with Harris County activists to bolster his plans. For instance, Curtis Graves, an up-and-coming African American leader, went to Austin to testify for Eckhardt's proposal, recommending a system that would finally bring representation to minorities.

Eckhardt was by no means the only Houston legislator with his eye on redistricting. Houston's Representative Paul Floyd, who opposed single-member districts, was the only Houston member on the redistricting committee; yet late in the session, Floyd complained that Harris County members "have purposely and systematically excluded me from any of the discussions."[17] Eckhardt became the de facto Harris County redistricting leader. For the state legislative districts, Eckhardt successfully struck a compromise with Mutscher's committee to have three multi-member state legislative districts, each within a congressional district (rather than one countywide district), with six or seven legislative seats inside each congressional district. Graves would later say that Eckhardt and others "worked to create a coalition of labor—white, Black, and Mexican American communities."[18] Building the coalition also produced candidates eager to buy into the proposal and join the legislature, including Graves.[19] For the congressional districts, Eckhardt wanted District 8 to include his residence, and Democratic Representative William Miller wanted to be in the redrawn District 7. Speaker Barnes and Chairman Mutscher agreed to this "Eckhardt-Miller" line.[20]

The resulting configuration created one district conceivably winnable by a Republican—though only 40 percent of the county's Republican voters were included in that district, with 30 percent of them in Thomas's District 8 and 30 percent in Casey's District 22.

Statewide, the House's congressional redistricting bill was consciously devised to protect conservative (mostly incumbent) Democrats. But Eckhardt supported it, since he got some of what he wanted, including a district he could run in effectively. He delicately approached his allies to tell them about the plan. He had to corral their votes for it and awkwardly confessed, "I sold out." Eckhardt's friends, though, laughed and responded, "Bob, if you get to Congress, it's worth it—we'll vote for it."[21]

The battle, of course, had just begun, with rancorous debate. In HB 67, the congressional redistricting bill, Dallas and Harris each gained one seat, east Texas lost a seat, and the at-large seat was eliminated. The House approved HB 67 by a vote of 118–24. In Harris County, the reconfigured 7th district had 417,283 residents, the 8th had 408,419, and the new 22nd had 417,396.[22] Eckhardt declared that the plan "fairly redistricts Harris County. We obtained these advantages above all other metropolitan counties: The county is divided in such a way as not to be linked with any other county. We lose no population to any outside district, and the districts are compact. . . . The problem of dividing our county in an equitable manner was made possible by harmonious action of the Harris County delegation and by the cooperation of Paul Floyd, the Harris County representative on the congressional and legislative districts committee."[23]

In HB 195, the Texas House redistricting bill, Harris gained seven seats (bringing the total to nineteen) and was the only county to be divided into districts. Dallas County gained five seats (up to fourteen), Bexar three, and Tarrant one. Across the rotunda, the redistricting bills kept coming up one vote shy of passing throughout May and the tensions mounted as senators sparred for advantage for themselves or their congressmen. Senator Spears objected to the congressional bill, saying, "This is a Mutscher-Mander."[24] Last-minute deals (claimed as "corrections") produced boundary changes, enlarging Wright Pat-man's rural east Texas congressional district, pairing two state representatives against each other, and making other alterations. The House approved the conference committee reports on much closer votes than the first time around, and the Senate gave its final approval by a vote of 18–13.[25]

In SB 547, the Senate redistricting bill, Harris County gained three seats, Dallas two, and Bexar one. Rural areas lost seats.[26] Dallas and Harris, for the first time, were divided into districts.[27] Harris County was configured into four single-member Senate districts and part of a fifth; Dallas County, three single-member districts. But the sausage-making produced such a mix of district types that Eckhardt argued (correctly, as would later be proven) that the use of four methods—single-member districts, multi-place districts in a county, multi-place districts within congressional districts, and flotorial state representative districts—would not pass judicial scrutiny.[28]

The Immediate Aftermath

On the last day of the session, twenty-six House members—including Eckhardt—filed a formal complaint against the congressional plan. The complaint charged that, overall, the plan violated *Gray v. Sanders*'s one person, one vote rule (in other areas of the state, the population differences were too great). Earlier plans in the legislature had variances of less than 7 percent; one had 2.3 percent. But the final version, after the horse trading and "corrections," had almost 19.4 percent variance. Bush and the Republicans, too, were dissatisfied, and filed suit. Still, on January 5, 1966, the Houston court unanimously upheld the plan. The three-judge panel wrote an exhaustive analysis of the redistricting plan and the politics that produced it. A concurring judge wrote that HB 67 was "the most discriminatory plan presented," but that "responsibility for redistricting rests with the legislature. Responsibility for the quality of the legislature rests with the people."[29]

The same members also objected to population variances in the state representative districts, which included flotorial districts.[30] Again, Bill Kilgarlin sued, and on February 2, 1966 (upheld in 1967), the court ruled in *Kilgarlin v. Hill* that the flotorial districts and population variances adopted for the House districts were unconstitutional. The legislature eliminated the flotorial districts in the 1967 session, and tweaked the districts again in 1969 to equalize population in the districts.[31]

Now, with the districts set, the races were on and history was being made. President Johnson's aide Jack Valenti had explored the possibility of a run for Albert Thomas's seat, but now demurred. Former LBJ Senate staffer John Wildenthal was interested in running for the new 7th district in west Houston. LBJ sent word to him that the Democrats could not win the seat—it was "locked" for George Bush. Wildenthal ran in the primary anyway and lost to District Attorney Frank Briscoe, who then lost to Bush.[32]

As for the racial and ethnic makeup of the new congressional districts, Houston's African American community was split up. The county's population was likely not large enough, even if reconfigured, to have produced a Black district in 1966, but Blacks' vote power was not significantly strengthened by the plan, either. More of the Black community was placed in District 8 than in the other two districts. Yet the 8th congressional district increased only from 24.7 percent Black to 26.0 percent.[33] Moreover, District 8 was composed of very segregated communities: Denver Harbor was overwhelmingly Latino, the Northeast and Acre Homes areas were overwhelmingly Black, and the rest of the district was majority white.

Barbara Jordan had run strong races for the state House in 1962 and 1964, but could not win with the countywide configuration and a dominant white voting population. With the smaller House districts after redistricting, there was finally a possibility for Blacks to win there. But she decided to aim higher, since the state Senate seats were now single-member districts and there was a district that was predominantly minority. Jordan ran for the state Senate nomination and won, making history in 1966

as the first African American in the Texas Senate since Reconstruction. The *Bush* and *Kilgarlin* lawsuits, coupled with Eckhardt's redistricting scheme and coalition building, helped bring
other African Americans to office in the Texas legislature in 1967
(Barbara Jordan in the Senate, and Curtis Graves, Joe Lockridge,
and Zan Holmes in the House). Jordan soon made it to Congress
in 1971 thanks to redistricting and the addition of yet another
Houston congressional seat.

Racial issues would also play a role in the newly created 7th
congressional district. Republican George Bush, having lost a
statewide race against Democrat Ralph Yarborough for the U.S.
Senate in November 1964, ran in 1966 for the new Houston
House seat that his lawsuit had helped create. Representative
Miller may have had a strong hand in drawing the district, but he
could not control the forces in the Democratic primary. District
Attorney Frank Briscoe ran for the congressional nomination
and Miller, instead, ran for state Senate and lost. The 7th congressional district had a Black population of only 15 percent, but
the Black community was particularly wary of Briscoe because
he had had a public role in indicting Black school board trustee
Mrs. Charles E. White.[34] Both Briscoe and Bush opposed open
housing legislation being debated in Congress, and in the 1964
race Bush had criticized Senator Ralph Yarborough for supporting the Civil Rights Act.[35] But in response to the Black community's anger at Briscoe's prosecution of Mrs. White, Bush made
subtle appeals to Blacks. Briscoe, in turn, accused Bush of "ap-
pealing to the Negro bloc." *Forward Times*, a leading Black news-
paper, had criticized Bush in 1964, but endorsed him against Briscoe. Bush got 34 percent of the Black vote and won the election.[36]

In the 8th district, Congressman Thomas died and his widow,
Lera, filled out his term. In the Democratic primary, Eckhardt
won 53 percent in a three-way race.[37] With no Republican opponent, Eckhardt won the seat in November. After this 1965 redistricting and increase in equalization of representation, Houston
ushered in a new era with two new Congressmen: its first labor-
Democratic congressman and its first Republican. Eckhardt went
to Bush's campaign office on election night to congratulate him.

They were both invited to College Station to speak at the Great Issues Committee Political Forum with Texas A&M students and faculty. They accepted and rode up together, getting to know each other better.[38]

Little could the pair know that Bush would serve but four years in the House, then take many detours that would lead him (and his son) to the White House. Eckhardt was beginning a long congressional career in which he played seminal roles in the nation's environmental, consumer protection, and war powers outcomes—then as he was serving as chair of the House's powerful Oversight and Investigations subcommittee in 1980, he was targeted by emerging New Right strategists as their number one House target and defeated just before redistricting could have altered his district. Barbara Jordan won her state Senate race and played a central role in the 1971 redistricting that gave Harris County a fourth congressional district, shaping a district for herself out of Eckhardt's, Bush's, and Casey's districts.

The Long-Range Aftermath of the 1965 Redistricting

Texas's 1965 redistricting institutionalized several dynamics that affected redistricting in the following decades. Now there were two-party competition, activated racial and ethnic groups, minimalized variance from population equality, immediate court challenges to the plans, and single-member districts. Not long after the historic 1965 mid-decade redistricting, the 1970 census triggered another round of legislative sausage-making. With courts now peering over the legislature's shoulder, legislators knew that they had to reward urban growth via state House and Senate redistricting. But in the midst of the swirling redistricting politics came the Sharpstown imbroglio that upended Texas politics. Gus Mutscher was now House Speaker, and while he and others in his leadership and staff team were under federal investigation, opponents inside the House (dubbed the Dirty Thirty) pressed for investigations. Mutscher's team produced district lines that forced members of the Dirty Thirty to run against one another or against the powerful House committee chairs, and rammed their plan through both chambers.[39]

The Senate redistricting plan failed to pass by the end of the session, and in September the Texas Supreme Court declared the House plan unconstitutional, thus activating the Legislative Redistricting Board to write both plans.[40] The board had heated differences over the issue of single-member districts. Land Commissioner Bob Armstrong (who had been a House member in 1965) preferred single-member districts in all urban areas. Lieutenant Governor Barnes opposed the board making new sub-county districts, because the legislature had not, although they had done so for Harris in 1965. The new plan approved by the Board created twenty-four single-member Harris County House districts (but no single-member districts elsewhere). As a member of the board, Speaker Mutscher had "strenuous objections" to the new House plan that the Legislative Redistricting Board approved in a 4–1 vote. Soon, litigation over the plan provided additional equalization breakthroughs: *Graves v. Barnes* (1972), *White v. Regester* (1973), and *Graves v. Barnes* (1974 and 1975) held that the at-large systems in urban counties diluted minority representation.[41]

Continued Texas population growth got Texas one new congressional seat in the 1970 reapportionment and a 24-district plan was enacted by the legislature in 1971. Harris won the new district even though the redrawn lines crossed the county boundaries. Ultimately, the plan was challenged and thrown out by the federal court reviewing it.[42] A new plan was ordered for the 1974 elections by the U.S. District Court for the Northern District of Texas (*White v. Weiser* 1973) to address minority voting rights issues. The plan was enacted by the legislature in 1975, with minor revisions.[43]

The blockbuster development, however, was the extension of the 1965 U.S. Voting Rights Act to Texas in 1975, and its coverage of language minorities—thereby bringing Latino voters under its purview. Application of the Act affected not only state legislative and congressional representation, but also representation schemes in local governance across the state. Both litigation and

Justice Department objections to voting system changes were extensive.[44]

It is clear from the example of the 1965 Texas redistricting that redistricting events are vital to the chances of the candidates from various political factions to win representation in the legislature or Congress. Redistricting in the 1960s made possible Bob Eckhardt's and George Bush's national careers, while redistricting and population shifts in the 1970s made possible Barbara Jordan's career, and ultimately hastened Eckhardt's defeat just before the 1981 redistricting could have saved him. Redistricting also ushered in the era of urban and minority representation, single-member districts, equal-sized legislative and congressional districts, two-party representation, and endless litigation. By 1981, Texas had a new reality: for the first time since 1874, there was a Republican governor (though the legislature remained Democratic). The decennial census had triggered redistricting in the legislature, but Governor Bill Clements vetoed the Senate plan and a federal court once again threw out the House plan. The task was left to the Legislative Redistricting Board.

In 1991, the legislature (with Democrat Ann Richards as governor and Democratic majorities in both chambers) redistricted in its regular session, following submission of the new decennial census figures, and those lines went into effect. However, by 1995, Texas Republicans were arguing that the district lines violated legal standards; to stave off the uncertain outcome of litigation, the legislature redrew some of the district lines.

In 2001, Texas faced yet another new political configuration: a Democratic House majority, a Republican Senate majority, and a Republican governor (Rick Perry, who had been sworn in as George W. Bush left to become president). The legislature failed to redistrict, so the now-Republican-dominated Legislative Redistricting Board was activated. The Board drew the lines for the legislature, while courts drew the congressional lines. With the LRB's new lines, in 2002 Republicans won both the Texas Senate and the Texas House for the first time in 130 years. So, in the following 2003 session, at the urging of Congressman Tom DeLay, who was from Texas and was the Republican leader in the U.S. House, the legislature reopened congressional districting. Democratic legislators fled to Oklahoma and New Mexico, breaking the quorums in the House and Senate to stop the bills, but after three special sessions, Republicans won the battle and drew new lines.[45] With those new lines, Republicans won six new congressional seats in Texas in 2004. However, in 2006 the U.S. Supreme Court threw out some of those new Texas congressional districts; a federal court then drew new lines. The stage was set for 2011.

CHAPTER 2

Legislating in the Thicket

CRAIG A. WASHINGTON

When I reflect on the years I spent in the Texas legislature and in Congress during redistricting sessions, there are two dominant themes that stand out for me (and I suspect for most legislators involved in redistricting). The first is that there are genuine philosophical and moral issues underlying redistricting. The second is that the internal legislative power dynamics paint the critical backdrop for redistricting. These are the themes that I want to address in the Texas redistricting escapades from the 1970s to the 1990s.

Redistricting is, first and foremost, a civil rights issue. American history is replete with examples of those inside the halls of power manipulating the levers of democracy to keep themselves in power and keep outsiders out. If those without economic, social, or political power are denied democratic participation, then the game is over. Voting rights, of course, are the bedrock of democratic power. Sometimes those in power have sought to keep out those who were poor; sometimes they have sought to keep out those who were female; sometimes they have sought to keep out those who were of non-majoritarian religions; and sometimes they have sought to keep out those who were dark skinned. The tools they have used for denying this basic civil right are legion and well known. They include prohibiting votes from those not wealthy enough to own or pay taxes on property; prohibiting votes from those who did not pay a tax on voting;

simply banning any voting by certain groups, such as Black citizens (e.g., white primaries), women, non-churchgoers, ex-felons; or by erecting barriers impossible to surmount, such as the infamous southern literacy tests, grandfather clauses, or bean-counting guesses aimed at disenfranchising African Americans.[1]

Where, then, does the drawing of legislative district lines fit into this civil rights picture? It fits into that toolbox. If the vote cannot be absolutely denied to those outside the power centers, then district lines (given that we do not use systems like proportional representation) can be drawn and redrawn in and around those groups to accomplish the desired goal—disenfranchisement. The Massachusetts legislature in Elbridge Gerry's day knew exactly what it was doing with its salamander-like, in-and-out, in-and-out line drawing: they sought to keep Gerry's party in and keep the outs out.

The particular group that is "out" may change from era to era, from state to state, but the dynamic of the "in group" drawing lines to keep itself in and the "other" out is a constant. The court cases cited throughout this volume are replete with passionate defenses of equal representation as essential to constitutional democracy, with words full of outrage at the disenfranchisement resulting from artful drawing of lines to "crack" communities apart or to "pack" them together to minimize or eliminate their representation. Redistricting stories told across the nation and throughout our history—from the original gerrymander all the way up to Tom DeLay's shenanigans—provide prima facie evidence that redistricting is too often a tool of disenfranchisement.

Ultimately, the civil rights argument comes down to this: how do people in a democracy get government to respond to them? Only if they can either elect people from their community of interest or have genuine influence over those elected can people achieve true democratic responsiveness. When people have influence on the governors (getting officials to respond to them), it produces real changes in their lives—on the levels of fire protection, police protection, infrastructure, social services, and, yes, protection of civil rights. When communities of interest are shut out of actual representation or their impact on representatives is marginalized, government responsiveness drops, services and protections are not provided, and people's lives suffer. This subject of redistricting may be considered by many a highbrow, academic subject, but in reality, it has very real, consequential effects on the lives of people.

The first dominant theme, then, involves these philosophical and moral issues underlying redistricting. I quite honestly do not know that I was aware of the civil rights dimensions of redistricting when I entered the Texas legislature as a naïve young man in 1973; after years of legislating, I came to understand the issues. The second dominant theme is that internal legislative power dynamics set the stage for redistricting. What I seek to accomplish in this chapter is to demonstrate how power works in the legislature, how those machinations play out in redistricting, and then how civil rights are advanced or impeded by those power dynamics.

Getting to Austin

First, some background on how I got to the legislature—not as autobiography, but as an introduction to the themes and personalities that emerged in the legislative process over this twenty- to thirty-year period.

When Mickey Leland, Benny Reyes, and I drove an old car up to the capitol after our elections in 1972, we were already political allies and great friends. But we didn't start out that way. When I was president of the student bar association at the Texas Southern University (TSU) School of Law, Mickey was an undergraduate and president of the student body. As events in the 1950s to 1970s demonstrated, Texas Southern and Prairie View A&M University—the two historically Black colleges in the Houston area—were often places where the violence of southern segregation played out with horrific outcomes. In 1967, when a student crossing Wheeler Street (the main thoroughfare through TSU) was hit by a car, Mickey and others led student protests and sit-ins and shut down classes to try to get safer car and pedestrian flows. We law students continued going to class, and Mickey and I had a face-to-face heated argument over the class boycott. I told him that the students were going to need lawyers to defend them and that we needed to get our law degrees in order to help. Soon police troops stormed in and all hell broke loose. Nearly 500 students were arrested, a policeman was killed—most likely by a ricocheting police bullet—and several students were indicted for murder. (Outside lawyers and a change of venue eventually got the charges dropped.[2]) There were other tense confrontations with the police, the community, and the university administration on various occasions regarding treatment of student organizations, plans to put in a trash dump, and plans for a Burger King, all of which brought race, segregation, and economic power issues to the fore.

Mickey and I worked together on these issues as student leaders. I began practicing law and Mickey kept organizing. As a result of the 1971 creation of single-member House districts— and an increase in the number of Houston seats—Mickey decided to run for the legislature and convinced Benny and me to jump in as well.

Watershed elections have long-term consequences. The Sharpstown Scandal of 1971 triggered the amazing election of 1972. The "reform" backlash against the legislative establishment, coupled with the single-member districts that the redistricting produced, brought a wave of new legislators to the 1973 session. The legislature was a different place, with more African American members, more Mexican Americans, more liberals, and more Republicans. And many of us who swept in then were still there (and joined by others like us) in the 1981 redistricting session. Moreover, the power battles that were spawned in the 1971/1973 sessions still rippled through the capitol in 1981. So, to fully understand redistricting in any one legislative session, you really have to recreate the power gears that were at work at the time, influenced by the earlier dynamics.

I don't know that I understood then that our emergence into legislative politics was possible only because of the work of our predecessor generation of African Americans, Mexican Americans, and progressive whites in legislative and redistricting politics: Barbara Jordan, Curtis Graves, Lauro Cruz, Bob Eckhardt, and Bill Kilgarlin in Houston; Joe Lockridge, Zan Holmes, and Oscar Mauzy in Dallas; Henry B. González and Franklin Spears in San Antonio; and others, I'm sure. Eckhardt had lost his battle for single-member districts in 1965, but won the compromise of three subdistricts in Harris County, which brought in the first wave of new, young legislators in 1966, including the first African American legislators since Reconstruction—Curtis Graves in a Houston subdistrict, Dallas's Joe Lockridge (succeeded by Zan Holmes after Lockridge's death) in the House, and Barbara Jordan in the Senate; it also set the table for single-member districts won by the 1971 power battles in the Legislative Redistricting Board and the domino lawsuits by Bill Kilgarlin and Curtis Graves,[3] leading to our elections in 1972. That watershed election opened the doors for African American representation with the election to the House of Sam Hudson, Eddie Bernice Johnson, and Paul Ragsdale from Dallas; G. J. Sutton from San Antonio; and Anthony Hall, Mickey Leland, and myself from Houston.

Of course, the redistricting sword can cut both ways. The Harris County single-member state Senate districts triggered in the 1965 redistricting brought Barbara Jordan to the Texas Senate. By 1971, Houston gained a new congressional seat. Senator Jordan was able to fashion a congressional district for the Black community of Houston and she ran for that seat. So what would happen with her Senate seat? Representative Curtis Graves wanted that seat. Yet the power dynamics in the Senate would not allow that to happen; Lieutenant Governor Ben Barnes, the more conservative senators, and business lobbyists reportedly determined that they would never draw a district that Curtis could win.[4] At the same time that the Senate (and House) created the new congressional district, they (and ultimately the LRB) drew the Senate lines to take away the majority Black Senate district. Shut out of the possibility of a Senate seat, Curtis decided to run for the congressional seat, against Barbara. This, of course, set up real tensions in our community in the midst of our own campaigns for the legislature. We all greatly respected Barbara Jordan, and the Harris County Council of Organizations made clear its support for her; yet I also liked Curtis and voiced my support for him. Barbara won and went on to her storied, but short, career in Congress as the first African American congresswoman from a southern state; Curtis's electoral career was over, just as mine began. Such is the personal impact of redistricting!

Learning the Ropes

Seventy-six of us (an unprecedented 50 percent of the House) were freshmen in January 1973. But though a legislature begins on a specific day in January and lasts for two years, it does not begin anew each time; rather, the rules, politics, personalities, and power blocs from earlier legislatures haunt and often direct the dynamics of the new session. So when I arrived in 1973, it was in a swirl of activity as legislators tried to hold on to what they had before or to oust the old power centers and bring in a new day. The internal campaign for the House speakership, known colloquially as the Speaker's Race, defines the Texas House. But it is not merely the months-long battle for the gavel—it is the power teams that sift out in that campaign that carry over into the ensuing sessions. The bribery scandal of 1971 not only swept out dozens of legislators, it also led to the ouster of the traditional leadership bloc. During the 1973 session and the 1974 constitutional convention, we were led by new Speaker Price Daniel, Jr. But Daniel, in a reform fervor, pledged to serve only one term as Speaker. So, of course, a Speaker's race immediately broke out and we were all caught up in the battles among the varying candidates. I first supported Representative Fred Head. When he dropped out, I had to choose between Representatives Carl Parker and Billy Wayne Clayton. This choice illustrates the personal aspect of legislative politics—and ultimately its influence on redistricting.

Carl Parker probably seemed like the natural choice for me to make. We were both from the coastal area, urban environs, and we aligned on many issues. But Bill Clayton—a west Texas farmer/rancher/businessman from the conservative faction of the Democratic Party—came to me and asked for my vote. When I told him that I could support someone who would listen to my input and give me a fair hearing on urban issues, he readily and genuinely agreed. I came to believe that Parker thought he already knew urban issues and did not need additional allies there. I threw my support to Clayton, we became great friends, and Clayton (who served as Speaker from 1975 through 1982) stayed true to his word to treat me and Houston fairly. I soon found myself chair of the Criminal Jurisprudence Committee, then the Human Services Committee, chair of the Black Caucus, leader of the Harris County delegation—and, by 1981, a member of the redistricting committee. Thus, I was able to influence redistricting outcomes from these seats inside the power structure.

My first real experience with redistricting came while I was in the House, but in my role as a lawyer rather than as a legislator. This is a common dynamic in the part-time Texas legislature—lawyer-legislators work on both the inside and the outside. Beginning in 1973, I served as attorney in the Leroy Moses case, along with Frumencio Reyes and Al Green, suing the City of Houston in the United States District Court for the Southern District of Texas to get single-member districts.[5] We argued that the at-large election system (and the annexation of white populations) diluted Black and Hispanic votes, violating the Constitution and the Voting Rights Act. In 1975, Congresswoman Barbara Jordan got the Voting Rights Act extended to cover Texas. This may be the most important civil rights victory that she won in her career. Its requirements for preclearance by the Justice Department dampened the shenanigans that were the rule of the day, such as changing voting locations so that nontraditional voters would not be able to vote. Voting rights are often an enforcement issue, and the VRA created legal weapons that we could use to enforce constitutional and statutory provisions for voting rights.

Ultimately the *Moses* suit and another, the *Mann* suit, were consolidated and the litigation went back and forth on appeal throughout the 1970s.[6] We were able to prove that services in minority communities were not only inadequate, but of grossly lower quality than those services in white communities. José Garza does a fine job in his chapter of demonstrating this same dynamic in other local redistricting cases in Texas. Making this record helped us convince the court that at-large elections provided benefits for the majority, to the detriment of those not in the majority. Houston has had an election system with most of the city council seats in single-member districts ever since then.

Sometimes local and state redistricting politics become entwined. In the legislature, we became accustomed to local business interests lobbying us to overrule local governance when they did not get their way with the local folk. In the 1970s, with increasing African American and Hispanic representation in the legislature, local groups that had lost out to the local power-brokers were able to turn the tables, coming to us to exert legislative pressure on behalf of civil rights. I became involved in the effort to win minority representation in Houston's school governance. This time, rather than donning my lawyer hat, I wore my legislative hat. I introduced a bill in 1975—and won its passage—requiring the Houston Independent School District to elect trustees in single-member districts.[7] As a result, from that time forward, the HISD has been more responsive to broad segments of the Houston community.

Another example of legal battles I was involved in over voting rights involved Prairie View A&M University in Waller County (just outside of Houston). With the constitutional extension of voting to 18-year-old citizens, coupled with the cascading cases forcing single-member districts locally and in the legislature, college students were emerging as a new voting bloc. Thus, in Waller County, this emergence had the potential of empowering more Black and young voters. The county voter registrar tried to stymie this development by requiring Prairie View students to swear that they intended to continue living in the county after graduation. Nonstudents, of course, were not asked such a question. This was not the first time that local officials had tried to block student voting. A north Texas case had made its way to U.S. District Judge William Wayne Justice's court in the Eastern District. I so admired Judge Justice that, when I passed the bar and began federal practice, I drove all the way to Tyler for the honor of being sworn in by him. Prairie View is in the Eastern District, so I tried to get the case before Judge Justice. He ultimately determined that he did not have the requisite jurisdiction. Fortunately, we were able to refile and won a 1978 federal court order prohibiting the registrar from treating the students differently from other Waller County voters. Amazingly, in the first decade of the 21st century, the issue has resurfaced, with new county officials seemingly oblivious to the court order; the U.S. Justice Department has opened an investigation of Waller County's compliance.

By the time my first redistricting session rolled around, then, I was a seasoned legislator and had a decade of practicing law under my belt. My good friend Mickey Leland, though, served only three terms and went on to Congress. Barbara Jordan retired from Congress due to health problems and Mickey ran for and won her seat in 1978. Mickey became my congressman, and a part of my job in the legislature was to protect that seat—still the only congressional seat held by an African American in Texas.

1981 Redistricting Politics in the Texas House

As we approached the redistricting session of 1981, we knew that the number of state legislative seats would remain constant but that Texas would likely gain congressional seats. (Ultimately, the census and apportionment added three new Texas congressional seats.) Several of us involved in the 1981 redistricting jousts would later find ourselves in the Texas Senate—Gonzalo Barrientos, David Cain, Gene Green, Chuy Hinojosa, Ted Lyon, Frank Madla, Rene Oliveira, Frank Tejeda, Hector Uribe, John Whitmire, and myself; and several of us also ended up in Congress—Gene Green, Ron Coleman, John Bryant, Frank Tejeda, myself, Senators Lloyd Doggett and Bill Sarpalius, and on the other partisan side, Tom DeLay. The session had its usual wild moments, and CBS showed them to the nation. Author Larry L. King followed up his 1978 play "Best Little Whorehouse in Texas" with his 1981 Emmy-award-winning "Best Little Statehouse in Texas," with CBS Reports. King described "the corridors of power" in the Texas legislature, focusing on redistricting in the House and interest rate hikes in the Senate.[8] Texas journalist Molly Ivins chimed in, writing about the Larry L. King report: "The beauty of the 'Lege' is that it always commits its disservices to the public interest with great style. The gang does not disappoint this go-round, even though it was a tame session—not one fistfight was recorded."[9]

Billy Wayne Clayton was in his fourth and final term as Speaker and appointed me Speaker Pro Tem as well as putting me on the Regions and Compacts Committee—the redistricting committee. He appointed rural Representative Tim Von Dohlen as the committee chair. Von Dohlen authored the House redistricting bill, HB 960, and the congressional redistricting bill, HB 1400. Clayton balanced the 19-member committee so that factional or partisan battles did not dominate the debates and outcome. One of his key Republican supporters, Bob Davis, was on the committee to defend the position that Republicans should gain substantial representation. Clayton let the local delegations work out their own squabbles. I was informally in charge of Harris County, with Brad Wright representing Houston Republicans on the committee. I was also serving as chair of the Black Caucus. Thus, I needed to make sure that the final product satisfied Harris County and satisfied African American members—and Speaker Clayton expected me to do so. I also knew that, for the ensuing litigation, you have to make sure you get a record in committee. You send up the perfect plan in committee, then when you lose the vote on it, send it up again as an amendment on the floor if you can. Then, in the courtroom, your lawyers have evidence that the legislature could have done the right thing in protecting voting rights, but chose not to.

Speaker Clayton served as a hands-on referee on redistricting when he had to, spreading the redistricting maps out on his table and getting into the nitty gritty details. CBS negotiated an agreement to get their cameras in the back offices of the capitol, and Larry L. King followed us around. The documentary shows the redistricting wheeling and dealing in the Speaker's office. When two legislators would simply not agree to changes, Clayton would choose one over the other and finalize the map. The documentary shows Clayton calling Austin's Representatives Gonzalo Barrientos and Wilhelmina Delco in to hash out their differences, down to the final block.

Congressman Mickey Leland, of course, was keen on keeping the lines of the 18th congressional district good for our community in HB 1400. Because of the Voting Rights Act and its mandate for no retrogression in minority representation, there was actually little chance that the district would be hurt—had the legislature tried to do so, the courts and the Justice Department would have stopped it. Still, Mickey came to Austin and helped remind everyone of the need for his district to remain viable.

The congressional bill did not pass, as Governor Clements pressed his agenda for maximum Republican gains, and a special session was called to rehash it in SB 1. Ultimately, the districts were battled out in the Justice Department and the courts, as David Richards describes in Chapter 3.

In Harris County, we had delegation meetings on the state legislative redistricting, but still did not have agreement until late in the session.[10] Frankly, I did not want to get our plan out early, because I knew that the knives would be sharpened and any agreement could be gutted. Harris County, of course, had grown since 1971. The growth was in the minority communities and in Republican neighborhoods. The delegation established an informal committee of Ed Emmett to represent Republicans, El Franco Lee to represent African Americans, Al Luna to represent Hispanics, and Ralph Wallace to represent white Democrats in negotiations. Emmett wanted to create one new Hispanic district, in a way that would ensure more Republican districts. He presented a plan that pitted Democratic Representative Paul Colbert against Republican Brad Wright and Democrats Ralph Wallace and Ron Wilson against each other, assuring the demise of two white Democrats and the election of an African American and a Republican—while also adding another Republican seat and a Hispanic seat. Representative Luna supported the plan, and tensions mounted.

Paul Moreno, chair of the Mexican American Caucus, and I, as chair of the Black Caucus, decided that our two caucuses should meet and talk through the tension. Thus, the first-ever joint meeting of the Black Caucus and Mexican American Caucus was held over redistricting. Representative Luna argued for the Emmett plan that would increase both minority and Republican representation. I argued the other side. This same dynamic came up in the congressional redistricting, as Governor Clements tried to force the creation of a new Black congressional district in Dallas so that Republicans could gain more districts on the outskirts.

Legislative battles ultimately come down to votes. The outcome is determined by who gets 50 percent—and Republican state legislators and congressmen consistently vote in ways that are opposite to the policy directions that both African Americans and Mexican Americans support. Thus, it made no sense to me—and still does not—to increase the number of Black or brown faces in the legislature or Congress, if the cost is a net increase in the number of legislative votes against African American and Mexican American interests. I love the idea of increased minority representation. I do not believe, though, that setting increased minority representation as the top goal is a smart strategic decision. Doing so allows for political mischief, such as Clements taking advantage of a golden opportunity to advance Republican representation by using the minority communities as a Trojan horse.[11]

Today we use the terms "Red" for Republican ("Bloody Red" for overwhelmingly Republican districts) and "Blue" for Democrats ("Deep Blue" for overwhelmingly Democratic districts). If we pack African Americans or Mexican Americans into Deep Blue districts and Republicans into Bloody Red districts, then take the "Purple" (mixed voting) communities that are Anglo and draw them into the Bloody Red districts—just enough to pull them back to Red, good dependable Republican districts—then we have a strict racial divide in representation. Whites are Republicans; minorities are Democrats. Why would any legislator or congressman not from a minority community then listen to any of our input? Why would we ever win a policy vote? Such a redistricting scheme guarantees that what little gains we have made in getting government to respond to our concerns will be gone. "Republicans are not our friends," I told the caucus members at our joint meeting, and I meant that to the end of bettering representation for our communities of interest.

Speaker Clayton soon called me and a few other Harris County representatives into his office to argue over the maps. I eventually got all the delegation Democrats to side with me, with the exception of Al Luna. We managed to redraw the lines so that none of us in Harris County had to run against one another. When I presented my plan to the committee, it was approved 10-3, with only Harris County Republican Brad Wright and two Dallas members voting against it.[12]

Redistricting was simply one of the issues that we were juggling for those 140 days. Legislators do not have the luxury of concentrating solely on one issue at a time but must go back and forth among numerous issues and bills simultaneously. Political logrolling and backscratching over redistricting was a constant during the session. On the floor, while we debated the legislation of the day, instructions from the Speaker filtered out across the floor, while informal redistricting conversations and negotiations permeated the session as the committee and backroom negotiations wound their way to completion. In the midst of the politicking, Dallas's Representative Paul Ragsdale discovered that false data had been slipped into the Dallas maps and he confronted Republican Bob Davis about it in front of Larry L. King's camera. King also quizzed Davis and Chairman Von Dohlen about it on camera, but no one would admit to the dirty trick, and Von Dohlen simply declared that it was embarrassing and wouldn't happen again, but he wasn't interested in hunting out the culprits.

None of us wanted a bloody redistricting battle on the floor. Speaker Clayton invited each member, individually, to come to his office, look at the committee's map of his or her district, and sign a statement supporting the district lines. There is a great scene in *The Best Little Statehouse* showing legislators trooping into the Speaker's office, one by one, to sign their pledges to the district lines. Thus, by the end of the work by the committee and the Speaker, the committee's work was accepted—ironclad support was expected and was gained from most. Only 26 of 150 voted against it on the House floor.

We had a House redistricting plan for the next decade. Or so we hoped. As David Richards describes in the following chapter, the litigation, governor's objections, Justice Department review, and Legislative Redistricting Board plans kicked in and it was three years later before the plans were finalized. But they were out of our hands sine die in June 1981.

1991 Redistricting Politics: Congress and the Legislature

I had already decided to run for the Texas Senate once the redistricting plans were settled, as Barbara Jordan's old Senate seat in Houston's African American community was to be restored. I ran unopposed and served in the Senate for the rest of the 1980s. I suppose that I expected to sharpen my redistricting political skills anew in the Senate in 1991, but tragedy struck and changed everything. Throughout the 1980s Mickey Leland chaired the House Select Committee on Hunger. In 1989, he was touring Ethiopia when his plane crashed, and he and everyone else on board was killed. I was sickened and I grieved for my friend, along with the rest of Houston's Black community. In the midst of our grief, though, the congressional seat had to be filled. Several African American leaders in Houston were interested, and I encouraged them to run. Soon, however, I did not like the way the field had shaped up and I decided to run. I did so and won in the runoff.

Thus, I found myself leaving the Senate that I had come to love and moving to Congress in late 1989. By the time the 1991 redistricting rolled around, then, I found myself in the new role as a congressman lobbying my old Texas legislative colleagues for good redistricting lines. Jack Brooks, Democrat from the Beaumont area and dean of the Texas delegation in Washington, coordinated our weekly luncheons in the Capitol. He put me in charge of monitoring redistricting in Austin, since I was the most recent arrival from the state legislature and had good contacts back there.

In 1991, Texas was to gain three new congressional seats, and the legislature ended up putting one in Dallas, one in Houston, and one in south Texas. But the dynamics were similar to the 1981 Clements dynamics, and the courts were now thoroughly Republicanized by Presidents Reagan and Bush. *Bush v. Vera* eventually struck down the plan as a racial gerrymander.[13]

Once again, the Voting Rights Act made my district safe. One question was whether we could expand African American and Mexican American representation in the Texas delegation; another was whether we could continue to defend the Democratic seats in the delegation. The priority was to save John Bryant, Martin Frost, Ron Coleman, and Mike Andrews. I returned to Austin and met at the Austin Club with the Black Caucus that I had chaired, working with the new round of African American legislators—especially Larry Evans and El Franco Lee. Ron Wilson was serving on the House Redistricting Committee, but we did not see eye to eye.

We managed to keep all those endangered Democratic seats (all of which were held by Anglos). We also created a new Hispanic-dominated district in San Antonio, won by State Senator Frank Tejeda; a Hispanic-influenced district in Houston, won by an Anglo state Senator, Gene Green, who still serves in that seat; and an African American-dominated district in Dallas, won by state Senator Eddie Bernice Johnson. All three were Democrats. Yes, it helped to have a Democratic legislature and a Democratic governor! In one sense, then, it is understandable that Republicans came to believe they had been gerrymandered out of representation they believed they deserved—and they played the game of payback with a vengeance when redistricting rolled around again.

Conclusion

As a Texas legislator, then congressman, I looked at redistricting as an extension of the battles against old school disenfranchisement—be it Louisiana's requirement that African Americans accurately count the number of beans in a jar to be able to vote, or the grandfather clauses, or literacy tests, or poll taxes. And now we have the new school disenfranchisement thrusts: so-called ballot security programs, voter identification requirements, and "voter fraud" initiatives. All of these seek to minimize votes from groups that do not typically support the in-power group. We call this "vote suppression."

Redistricting can seem, on the surface, to be purely a game of partisan payback. But we know from the history of redistricting, from academic studies of redistricting, and from court documented situations that redistricting outcomes can either enfranchise or disenfranchise groups—deliberately or inadvertently. The Voting Rights Act exists to be used as a watchdog over the internal legislative party battles, alerting citizens and courts to dangerous civil rights violations—disenfranchisement—that can occur if the partisan knife fights in the legislature are allowed to go un-refereed. The battles in the Texas legislature demonstrate that we must understand the internal legislative power dynamics—and know who is at the power table in the redistricting battles—to fully comprehend the consequences of redistricting for citizens in a democracy.

CHAPTER 3

Litigating Texas Redistricting:
A Democratic Lawyer's Experience

DAVID R. RICHARDS

Redistricting as carried out in Texas is nothing more than a battle over allocation of power, with no suggestion that the Marquis of Queensbury rules attach. As the opening chapter demonstrates, redistricting came to the fore beginning in the 1960s with the first involvement of the federal courts implementing the notion of one person, one vote. The Supreme Court's announcement of this equal representation principle put to rest historical precedent that treated redistricting as a "political question" beyond the reach of the judiciary.

My interest in redistricting sprang from two related sources. First, as a Dallas-area lawyer, political organizer, and strategist, I saw how redistricting outcomes tilted the playing field in favor of those with power. I especially wanted to see African Americans get a foothold in the political arena, as they had been disenfranchised for so long. Second, as an Austin lawyer, I jumped into the post-*Baker* litigation arenas to battle for judicial victories in redistricting after the legislature had produced its convoluted (and all too often unconstitutional) districting schemes. Even in those court battles, the economic and political power players flexed their muscles, but at least those of us on the other side had a second shot at equality and fair representation. In this chapter, I seek to flesh out some of the litigation and political skirmishes that produced the redistricting plans we all have had to live with.

Politicking and Litigating the 1970s Districts

The opening salvos of the 1970s redistricting were launched by two venerable figures of Texas politics, State Representative Tom Craddick (R-Midland) and State Senator Oscar Mauzy (D-Dallas), who came from the absolute opposite ends of the political spectrum of Texas. The Texas legislature in its 1971 session had adopted an apportionment plan for Congress and for the Texas House, but failed to reapportion the Texas Senate.

The House plan was successfully attacked by Tom Craddick in *Craddick v. Smith*.[1] The Texas Supreme Court found that the "wholesale cutting" of county lines violated the Texas constitutional requirement of preservation of county lines in the apportionment process. The court's decision engrafted onto the county line rule the following admonition: "The only impairment of the mandate is that a county may be divided if to do so is necessary in order to comply with the equal population requirement of the Fourteenth Amendment."

The Texas Constitution provides for the convening of the Legislative Redistricting Board (LRB) in the event of the legislature's failure to apportion following the census. The Board had been convened to redistrict the Texas Senate but refused to undertake the task of redrawing House seats following the decision in the *Craddick* case. Senator Mauzy sued to compel the Board to act on House redistricting. In *Mauzy v. Redistricting Board*,[2] the Texas Supreme Court ordered the Board to proceed, noting that the constitutional provision creating the Board in 1948 had the "object and purpose . . . to get on with the job of legislative redistricting which had been neglected or purposely avoided for more than twenty-five years." Thus the stage was set for the redistricting of the Texas House.

The Board consisted of Lieutenant Governor Ben Barnes, the dominant force on the Board; Attorney General Crawford Martin, an establishment errand boy; Speaker Gus Mutscher, troubled by the Sharpstown scandal; Comptroller Robert Calvert, headed toward senility; and Land Commissioner Bob Armstrong, sole progressive on the Board. All were Democrats.

The dominant issue at the moment was the struggle for single-member House of Representatives districts in the urban areas. It was paramount in the Black and Hispanic political communities as well as in Republican circles. It was seen as the only way to break the stranglehold of the old-line conservative white Democrats. The issue had been raised in the 1960s litigation when the Harris County delegation had been divided into three subdistricts. At that time the state of Texas advised the federal court that state policy dictated that any time a county's population reached 1,000,000, the county's state House delegation would be carved into districts.

The 1970 census reflected that Dallas County now exceeded 1,300,000 in population, and the county had been allocated 18 seats in the Texas House. The LRB actually held hearings on redistricting, with Senator Mauzy presenting testimony demonstrating community support for single-member districts in Dallas County. Yet when the Board published its plan, Harris County had been divided into single-member districts and Dallas, along with the other urban counties, retained countywide elections. No credible explanation was ever offered for this anomalous treatment of the urban areas. When the Board members were deposed in ensuing litigation, they claimed that they had never discussed the issue of single-member districts in Dallas and left it to staff to decide. Staff members testified that they were waiting for instructions from the Board concerning the treatment of the single-member district question. Not particularly persuasive testimony! The reality was that the dominant business lobby preferred to deal with a slew of conservatives from Dallas and other cities (electable from at-large elections), but were somewhat afraid that at-large elections in Harris County might result in a sweep by the "Harris County Democrats," a liberal grassroots organization that had been winning elections. This surely explains the differing treatment of the urban centers.

Suits were filed instantly. We sued in Tyler in order to place our case in front of U.S. District Judge William Wayne Justice; this was coordinated with MALDEF (Mexican American Legal Defense and Educational Fund), which immediately intervened.

A group of conservative Democrats filed an identical suit in Dallas, hoping to secure a Dallas federal judge. State Representative Curtis Graves filed suit in Houston to challenge the Senate plan, which eviscerated the seat then held by Barbara Jordan, and a group of Republicans led by Van Henry Archer sued in San Antonio claiming a political gerrymander in the Bexar County Senate seats. After some pretrial skirmishing, all of the cases were consolidated in front of a three-judge federal court consisting of Fifth Circuit Judge Irving Goldberg and District Judges Justice and John R. Wood of San Antonio.

The case went to trial two months later in January. There were so many lawyers that it was hard to fit them into the courtroom. By trial time the single-member district challenge was pared down to Dallas and Bexar Counties. Ed Idar, Jr., and George Korbel represented MALDEF and carried the burden of the Bexar challenge. Tom Gee, later of the Fifth Circuit, and Jim George, representing the state Republican Party, joined in the challenge to the at-large elections. My old law partner John Collins of Dallas helped me pull together the Dallas challenge. Leon Jaworski of Fulbright-Jaworski led the state's defense, along with a smattering of assistant attorneys general. Folded in were the Graves and Archer challenges.

The court moved more swiftly than we had anticipated. In *Graves v. Barnes*, it rolled back the deadlines for filing for office, issued a 70-page opinion invalidating the at-large elections in Dallas and Bexar, and put into place our proposed single-member districts in those counties for the 1972 elections.[3] Once the dust settled and the cries and shouts subsided, a small revolution occurred in the Texas House of Representatives. The single-member district elections in Harris, Dallas, and Bexar produced—among others—Senfronia Thompson, Craig Washington, Mickey Leland, and Ben Reyes from Houston; Paul Ragsdale, Eddie Bernice Johnson, and Jim Mattox from Dallas; G. J. Sutton and Matt Garcia from San Antonio—minorities and progressives, none of whom, I venture, could have been elected countywide.

One of the more endearing tales from these victories chronicles the arrival of Mickey Leland, Craig Washington, and Ben Reyes at the state capitol. They drove up together from Houston in some clunker of a vehicle and began to circle the capitol grounds looking for a parking place. One of the omnipresent attendants approached the vehicle and inquired, "What you boys looking for?" They explained that they were looking for parking, and the quick response was, "These places are reserved for members of the Texas Legislature"—to which Craig replied, "Well boss, we'uns is members of the Texas Legislature."

The challenges to the Senate redistricting plan failed, although Judge Justice in dissent argued that the LRB plan for Houston operated "to fragment the inner city Black voters into four districts" and was a racial gerrymander. Barbara Jordan was leaving her Senate seat and moving on to Congress in a newly created Harris County congressional district, and Harris County did not elect another African American senator until the 1980s, with Craig Washington's election.

Before the decade was over we tried the second round of the *Regester* case and again the Court ordered single-member districts for the balance of the state's urban counties.[4] By the 1974 elections, partly by way of settlement, there were no more multi-member legislative districts, and counties such as Tarrant and Travis began to elect from single-member districts. The end result was a continuing increase in the number of minorities elected to the legislature, as well as the number of Republicans. The essentially all white, all Democratic Texas House of Representatives was no more.

A second case from Texas, *White v. Weiser*, went to the Supreme Court following the 1970 census.[5] This suit was brought by Dan Weiser, a long-time progressive activist in Dallas, and challenged the congressional redistricting plan adopted by the Texas legislature. Constitutional law scholar Charles Black of the Yale law faculty argued the *Weiser* case on behalf of the state. He was brought into the case at the urging of his childhood friend, Houston Congressman Bob Eckhardt, the two of them having grown up together in Austin.

The *Weiser* and *Regester* cases were argued back-to-back on the same day before the U.S. Supreme Court, and taken together they stand for several propositions that are still operative today. With respect to congressional redistricting, the Court will insist upon essentially no population disparity between the districts. The Supreme Court rejected the congressional plan even though the average deviation between the districts was less than 1 percent. The district with the largest deviation was 2.43 percent over the ideal. In the Court's words in *Kirkpatrick v. Preisler* the Constitution will "permit only those population variances among congressional districts that 'are unavoidable despite a good-faith effort to achieve absolute equality. . .'"[6] In contrast, the Court in *Regester* dealt with deviation issues in the Texas House of Representatives, found tolerable a total deviation of 9.9 percent, and opined that the states were entitled to greater leeway when redistricting their own legislative bodies. As a result of this ruling it became fairly common thereafter for state legislative bodies to assume that they could pass constitutional muster if they produced a plan with no more than a 10 percent deviation. Finally, the Supreme Court in *Weiser* spoke to the issue of the role of federal courts in fashioning their own redistricting plans when confronted with a failed state enactment. In *Weiser*, elections were on the horizon and there was no constitutional plan in place, so it fell upon the trial court to impose a plan for the immediate election. In developing such plans the trial court "should not preempt the legislative task [of reapportionment] nor intrude upon state policy any more than necessary." By mid-decade the litigation was concluded, and the elective districts were in place for the House, Senate, and Congress.

Politicking and Litigating the 1980s Districts

By the time of the 1980 census, technology had taken over the redistricting process. In the 1970s we were drawing districts on the kitchen table with felt markers. By 1980 computers had arrived, forever changing the mechanical process of redistricting, but not, of course, the politics of the game. By 1980 we had two additional dramatic changes: application of the Voting Rights Act to Texas, and a Republican governor in the person of Bill Clements, who was determined to play a major role in the process.

The Texas House and Senate both managed to pass redistricting plans in the regular legislative session though neither were destined for a very long life. Governor Clements vetoed the Senate plan. A suit was filed to challenge the House plan on the basis that it violated the Texas Constitution, Article 3, Section 26, by unnecessarily cutting county lines. In *Clements v. Valles*[7] the Texas Supreme Court agreed and enjoined elections under the House-adopted redistricting plan. So once again the Legislative Redistricting Board was called into action. The players this round were once again Land Commissioner Armstrong and Lieutenant Governor Barnes, with newcomers Attorney General Mark White, House Speaker Billy Clayton, and Comptroller Bob Bullock. By now Texas was covered by Section 5 of the Voting Rights Act (by virtue of the 1975 amendments to the Act). The U.S. Department of Justice (DOJ) managed to find objections to all of the plans adopted by the LRB, and litigation ensued. The real fireworks, however, emerged from the congressional redistricting process.

The governor, suddenly a convert to race sensitivity, insisted that there be created in Dallas a majority Black congressional district. The reality was that the Black population was not sufficient at that time to create such a district. The truth was that Governor Clements was determined to eliminate the congressional seat then held by Democrat Jim Mattox. Mattox had won the seat in a bruising race against Republican stalwart Tom Pauken, and had become public enemy number one for Dallas Republicans. It took a special session and a prolonged battle, but Clements finally got his way, despite the opposition of almost every minority member of the legislature. Shortly thereafter Mattox showed up at my office and prevailed upon me to file suit to challenge the congressional plan. I had no difficulty securing Black leaders in Dallas to join as plaintiffs.

The congressional suit was heard by a three-judge court consisting of William Wayne Justice, District Judge Robert Parker, and 5th Circuit Judge Sam Johnson. The Court rolled back the filing deadlines for congressional seats but left in place the deadlines for all other offices. Shortly before the case went to trial Mattox came to me and wanted to know whether I was going to win the case. I told him I had no idea, for it was a most difficult case. Our basic claim was that the Dallas portion of the plan was a racial gerrymander, allegedly benign but ineffective to enhance minority voting strength, and in any event any such gerrymander must be supported by a compelling state interest. Mattox was not happy and announced that if I could not assure a victory, he was going to file for Attorney General of Texas. Shortly later he filed for Attorney General, leaving me with a lawsuit to be tried.

The trial court ruled with me and implemented a modified congressional plan for the Dallas area. I thought I was home free and then, in *Seamon v. Upham*, the U.S. Supreme Court sent the plan back with instructions that the trial court should determine whether it was too late to reinstitute the state plan.[8] By now it was well into April and the May primaries loomed. The trial court concluded that it was too late to change the election boundaries and directed that the elections be held under their plan. Johnny Bryant won election to the old Mattox seat and the Texas legislature later confirmed that court plan as the permanent plan for the decade.

While we were flailing around with the congressional case there were parallel proceedings concerning the House and Senate redistricting plans. The Legislative Redistricting Board had adopted House and Senate plans. Predictably suits were promptly filed attacking the plans, in this instance primarily by Republican interests. The cases were ultimately consolidated in a cause styled *Terrazas v. Clements*,[9] before federal judges Randall, Jerry Buchmeyer, and Barefoot Sanders. With Section 5 of the Voting Rights Act in place, none of the plans could be implemented until precleared by the Justice Department. Here again Governor Clements raised his head. On November 23, 1981, Attorney General White, who had been designated by the LRB to make the DOJ submission, submitted the plans and urged DOJ approval. A week later, Governor Clements's secretary of state made his submission with the notation that "the submitted Plan may not comply with Voting Rights Act . . . "

Thus the political warfare continued. With the governor sandbagging the redistricting plans it was no surprise that a Republican Justice Department interposed objections to the plans. The effect of the objections was to prevent elections under the new plans and to require the federal court to adopt interim election plans for the 1982 Texas House and Senate.

The court chose to implement the LRB plans except in the areas that drew Justice Department objections. (Those objections were confined to Dallas, Bexar, and El Paso for the House, and Harris and Bexar for the Senate.) In Bexar and El Paso the Court adopted the MALDEF proposals, but in Dallas County the Court concluded that the proposed modifications were so extensive that timely elections could not be conducted and, as a result, implemented the LRB plan. With respect to the Senate, the Court rejected all of the alternative plans presented and kept in place the LRB plans for both Harris and Bexar as interim plans for the 1982 elections. The Court was much troubled by the extensive changes required by the rejected alternatives and the difficulties in attempting to conduct the May primary elections in an orderly fashion—the same concern that had confronted the court hearing that year's congressional case.

By the end of 1982 Jim Mattox had been elected Attorney General of Texas and I had been hired as Executive Assistant Attorney General to take charge of the state's litigation. One of my first chores was to sort out the issues remaining from the previous year's redistricting litigation. With Governor Clements gone and Mark White in the governor's mansion, resolution of these lingering questions became much simpler.

The incoming legislature adopted a congressional redistricting that left in place the Court's Dallas configuration and adopted minor changes elsewhere. The governor signed the bill, it was precleared by the Justice Department, and it governed the congressional elections for the balance of the 1980s.

The Senate presented somewhat trickier questions. In accordance with Texas law, the entire 31 members of the Senate were elected in 1982. Lots were then drawn to determine which of the newly elected senators would receive four-year terms and which only two-year terms. In order to satisfy the Justice Department, modifications had to be made in the Senate plan. If the modifications were embodied in a new redistricting plan, under Texas law this would result in the entire Senate being forced to run again in 1984. For those senators who had drawn the four-year terms, this was an unthinkable result. After protracted negotiations, a modified Senate plan was created that satisfied MALDEF and the Justice Department. One result of the new Senate map was the reestablishment of the old Barbara Jordan Senate seat and the election of Craig Washington to the Texas Senate. Rather than adopt the modified plan as legislation, the Senate passed a resolution urging the federal court to adopt the settlement plan for the future senatorial elections. Attorney General Mattox issued an opinion letter concluding that this procedure would not require the entire Senate to run again in 1984.

The proposed resolution of the Senate issues was presented to the three-judge court sitting in the *Terrazas* case in the form of a proposed consent decree. The motion to approve the consent decree was joined by the MALDEF plaintiffs and was approved by the court in a lengthy order. Among the court's findings:

> This Court finds that the requirement of Section 25, Article III of the Texas Constitution providing for the division of the State into senatorial districts according to the number of qualified electors rather than population dilutes the voting strength of racial and ethnic minorities and discriminates against racial and ethnic minorities in violation of the Fourteenth and Fifteenth Amendments to the United States Constitution and Section 2 of the Voting Rights Act.[10]

Finally, in January 1984, the last remaining issue was put to rest. MALDEF had challenged the configurations of the Texas House seats in Dallas County, arguing that the lines fragmented the Hispanic community in Dallas and foreclosed that community from meaningful opportunity to elect a candidate of its choice. The three-judge court rejected the argument and upheld the House plan in one more exhaustive opinion.[11] In that case I found myself on the side of the state defending the Dallas map against my dear friend José Garza representing MALDEF. I suppose one just learns to play it as it lays.

Politicking and Litigating the 1990s Districts

When the 1990 census rolled around, there was a Democrat in the governor's office (Ann Richards), Democrat Dan Morales as attorney general, and Democrats handily in control of the legislative branch, with Bob Bullock as lieutenant governor (Senate president) and Gib Lewis as House Speaker. Rick Gray and I got hired to represent the legislative interests represented by Bullock and Lewis. This should have been a piece of cake, but there's many a slip between the cup and the lip.

The mother's milk of redistricting lawsuits is forum shopping—that is, seeking the most favorable judicial setting for the ultimate litigation. Typically these cases are filed before there is really anything in controversy; essentially, placeholder suits. Two such cases arose in 1991. In February 1991 Hispanic plaintiffs filed a state court suit in Hidalgo County, styled *Mena v. Richards*, alleging a census undercount of Hispanics. In May 1991, before new plans existed, Republican interests filed in the federal court in Austin before James Nowlin, in *Terrazas v. Slagle*, alleging unconstitutionality of the redistricting plans. (Nowlin, a former Texas Republican legislator, soon became more than just a judge in the proceedings, as we shall see.)

The looming primary elections of 1992 dictated the central dynamic of the early legal skirmishing. Candidates must file for a place on the primary ballot no later than January 2 for the March primary elections. Census data generally becomes available in March, while the legislature is in session, typically leaving the legislature some three months to enact redistricting plans. In 1991 the legislature adopted redistricting plans for the Texas House and Senate but failed to enact a congressional plan. However, a special session produced a new congressional plan. Now came the time to deal with the remaining hurdles for implementation: the pending litigation and preclearance by the Justice Department. DOJ preclearance can be frustrating. First, the burden is upon the submitting body to persuade that the proposed plans do not retrogress minority voting strength, a concept that is not entirely clear-cut. The material required for submission can be voluminous, including all the decade's previous election returns. Although the statute requires the department to act within 60 days of submission, if the DOJ requests additional data an automatic 60-day extension is imposed. Finally, objection to any portion of a plan prevents implementation of the plan as a whole. The strategy to deal with this dynamic was well settled by the 1990s: pick a favorable forum and hope to delay DOJ action long enough to be able to invoke the power of your chosen court to impose an interim election plan for the immediate upcoming elections. As we discuss later, the Republican strategy in the federal court worked quite well, at least initially.

While Republicans were cementing their position in the federal system (with George Bush now as president), Hispanic plaintiffs were whacking away in the state courts. The state court lawsuits resulted in settlement agreements between the state defendants, the governor, and the attorney general. The settlements modified the legislatively enacted reapportionment plans for the Texas House and Senate. These settlements were approved in the Hidalgo County cases styled *Mena v. Richards* and *Quiroz v. Richards*.[12] There is simply no way to fully explain all of the maneuvering that produced these settlements; suffice it to say that the Republicans were infuriated by the settlement agreements, and the plaintiffs in the federal action brought an original mandamus proceeding in the Texas Supreme Court to prevent implementation of the settlements.

In *Terrazas v. Ramirez*, issued on December 17, 1991, the Texas Supreme Court blocked the settlement agreements from being utilized for the upcoming primary elections.[13] The opinion was probably the most vitriolic in the Court's history, as Justice Nathan Hecht for the majority and Oscar Mauzy (who had left the Senate and was elected as a justice) in dissent inveighed against each another. Among other participants in the decision were Justice (now U.S. Senator) John Cornyn joining Justice Hecht's majority opinion and Justice (now Congressman) Lloyd Doggett joining Justice Mauzy in dissent. The essential theory of the ruling is that the *Terrazas* parties were denied due process because they were not participants in the trial court's hearings on the development of the settlement plans.

The effect of the Texas Supreme Court decision was to free up the federal court to move forward with its pending case. On December 24, 1991, in *Terrazas v. Slagle*, the three-judge federal court imposed its own interim election plan for the Texas House and Senate, leaving undisturbed the congressional apportionment plan.[14] Not too surprisingly the Court plan was tilted in favor of Republican interests. Now, there is a somewhat spicy backchannel tale. While the matter was pending before the federal court, I received a nighttime phone call reporting that Judge Nowlin's law clerks were meeting with a Republican legislator and drafting redistricting plans in the state's computer system. The next day, after further investigation, I reported this to our client, Lieutenant Governor Bullock, who readily agreed that we should promptly move to recuse Judge Nowlin and perhaps derail the Court's effort to redraw the state map. A confrontation between Bullock and Attorney General Dan Morales ensued. Morales refused to move for recusal and fired me, as a state's lawyer in the matter, and the court plan duly issued and became the election plan for the 1992 elections.

Of course, this was not the end of matters. Governor Ann Richards called a special session to address House and Senate redistricting. The legislature adopted new plans essentially mirroring the settlement plans that had emerged from the settlement in *Mena v. Richards*. This triggered an entirely new round of litigation. First, back to the three-judge court sitting in Austin in the *Terrazas* lawsuit: by now Judge Nowlin had stepped aside and had been replaced by Judge Harry Lee Hudspeth. The state successfully defended the House and Senate plans in this round. Now came the preclearance question. The state, leery of the Republican Justice Department, bypassed the Department and filed directly before a three-judge court in the District of Columbia an alternative means of securing preclearance under section 5 of the Voting Rights Act.

The state's D.C. lawsuit sought preclearance of all plans from the House, Senate, Congress, and State Board of Education. Ultimately only the Senate plan was contested by Republican intervenors who had been parties in the endless *Terrazas* litigation in the Texas courts. In 1992 the D.C. court gave approval to all of the plans and everyone could draw a big sigh of relief. But wait! Perhaps the story continues.

A new lawsuit was filed challenging the congressional plan on the grounds that it constituted a racial gerrymander. Texas had been allocated three new congressional seats based on the 1990 census. The legislature set about creating three new minority seats in Dallas, Houston, and South Texas, and reconfigured a Houston seat to increase its African American percentages. One suspects that this was in part a result of prodding by the Department of Justice, as they were wont in this era to push for maximizing minority representation. Because of Texas computer technology the districts could be—and were—drawn on racial lines, and all resembled Rorschach inkblots with fingers running in all directions. The federal trial court struck down three of the districts, but the Supreme Court stayed the order, and the state's existing plan was the basis for the 1994 elections.

In June of 1996 the Supreme Court issued its opinion in *Bush v. Vera*, affirming the trial court and declaring unconstitutional three of the congressional districts.[15] The Court held that these districts were drawn with race as the predominant factor, and such racial line drawing, even if benign, violated the Equal Protection Clause of the 14th Amendment. This was precisely the reasoning of Judge Justice a decade earlier in *Seamon v. Upham*, invalidating the 1980 congressional redistricting in Dallas County. On remand from the Supreme Court, the trial court in *Vera* blew aside any deference to state election processes, redrawing the disputed districts and those adjoining. It went further and ordered a special primary in the redrawn districts to be held in conjunction with the November general election and runoffs to be held in December 1996. Later, when the legislature did not enact a new congressional plan, the trial court ordered its plan to remain in effect indefinitely.

The decade staggered to a close with a new lawsuit challenging the House and Senate plans as racial gerrymanders. It was settled with modified plans for the Senate. This, of course, triggered a question of whether this was a redistricting plan that would shorten Senate terms and require the entire Senate to run again. Senators sued seeking a declaration that settlement would not require all of them to immediately run again, and prevailed in *Armbrister v. Morales*.[16] Seven years deep into litigation we could finally put to rest redistricting based on the 1990 census.

Politicking and Litigating in the New Century

These early redistricting years were simply a warm-up for the 2000 round, a round that could appropriately be labeled the Tom DeLay decade of redistricting. As this is being written there are still pending criminal cases as an outgrowth of this tempestuous struggle. For a thorough treatment of the subject, see Steve Bickerstaff's excellent source *Lines in the Sand: Congressional Redistricting in Texas and the Downfall of Tom DeLay*.[17]

The 77th Legislature (2001) was divided. Democrat Pete Laney was Speaker of the Texas House. George W. Bush had been elected president and Republican Lieutenant Governor Rick Perry had assumed the governorship. The Texas Senate was controlled by Republicans, and State Senator Bill Ratliff had been chosen by the Senate to fill Perry's place as presiding officer. The legislature was unable to produce redistricting plans for the House, Senate, State Board of Education, or Congress, and the new census had allocated two additional congressional seats to Texas. This was a fine kettle of fish and the lawyers were ready.

Apportionment of the House and Senate headed to the Legislative Redistricting Board. Congressional issues headed to a half-dozen or more lawsuits scattered across Texas in both federal and state courts, and the State Board issues ended up in federal court in a somewhat more restrained proceeding. First, the LRB process.

In 2001 the LRB was composed of Bill Ratliff, Attorney General John Cornyn, Speaker Laney, Comptroller Carol Rylander, and Land Commissioner David Dewhurst. With Laney as the only Democrat, the Board was safely under Republican control. Although Ratliff attempted to inject a moderating influence, he was outvoted by the Republican stalwarts, and the House and Senate plans were a testimony to political gerrymandering. Indeed the principal architect was Jim Ellis, a staffer for U.S. House Majority Leader (and former Texas legislator) Tom DeLay. The gerrymander was the first step in DeLay's long-range plan for the Texas congressional seats. First, he had to control both houses of the Texas legislature and specifically the Speaker of the Texas House. Tom Craddick reappeared out of the past as the preferred candidate for the DeLay operation.

DeLay's fundraising mechanism went into full swing and focused on taking control of the Texas House. DeLay created an organization known as Texans for a Republican Majority (TRMPAC) to collect and funnel money into selected Texas House races. His efforts were much aided by Bill Hammond and the Texas Association of Business (TAB). Between the two operations hundreds of thousands of dollars were raised and spent in the 2002 election cycle for the Texas House of Representatives, producing a Republican majority with Tom Craddick as Speaker.

After the 2002 elections, it became apparent that an unprecedented amount of money had poured into Texas House races, much of which had not been reported to the Texas Ethics Commission as required by Texas law. The principal culprit appeared to be Congressman DeLay's TRMPAC. The Texas Election Code affords a private right of action to candidates who have been targeted by unreported political contributions, with the claim running against the designated treasurer of the political committee. Bill Ceverha of Dallas, a longtime Republican political player and former legislator, was the designated treasurer of TRMPAC. Joe Crews, Chris Feldman, and I filed suit against

Ceverha on behalf of five losing Democratic House candidates (Paul Clayton, Mike Head, David Lengefeld, Ann Kitchen, and Danny Duncan). In May 2005, Judge Joe Hart of Austin ruled for the plaintiffs—finding they had been targeted by unreported corporate political contributions and awarding damages and attorney's fees against Ceverha. Ceverha filed for bankruptcy and the case was ultimately settled through the bankruptcy court.

Of course, it was the TRMPAC operation that resulted in DeLay's indictment and ultimate conviction for money laundering—washing corporate funds into political campaigns in violation of Texas law—a matter still on appeal. Much of the evidence developed in this trial formed the basis for DeLay's indictment and later conviction. But, of course, by then the electoral damage had been done and the Texas Congressional delegation had been elected under the DeLay redistricting scheme.

While the politics played out, the redistricting litigation had been well underway with differing results. Democratic strategists filed early in the Eastern District of Texas. Seeking to fix a venue for all of the ensuing litigation, they drew a three-judge federal court consisting of district judges John Hannah and John Ward, both Democrats, and Patrick Higginbotham from the 5th Circuit Court of Appeals. All of the challenges were ultimately consolidated, and this court ended up overseeing all of the challenges to the House, Senate, and congressional plans. There were many steps in that process, and much lawyer time burned up before it all came to rest with the court issuing a series of opinions in *Balderas v. State of Texas*.[18]

The Senate proved to be the least troublesome for the state. In October 2001 the Department of Justice gave preclearance to the Senate plan and in November the court rejected the challenges to the plan, holding: "We cannot say that this plan, which satisfies the Voting Rights Act and contains less than 10% deviation is so without reason as to violate the Equal Protection Clause. It is plainly the product of partisan line-drawing."

With respect to the Texas House, the court issued its opinion on the same day as the Senate decision. In the case of the House, the Justice Department had raised objection to districts in Bexar County and south Texas on the grounds that Latino voting interests had been adversely affected by the LRB plan. The Court, as it had in the Senate case, rejected all of the constitutional and statutory attacks on the plan and confined its remedy to the specific districts that had been singled out by the Justice Department. An interim plan was put in place that modified the designated districts, and the 2002 Texas legislative elections went forward basically under the DeLay scheme.

Congressional elections took a somewhat different course. After the Texas Supreme Court invalidated the congressional plan formulated by the Travis County District Court, the matter moved back to the federal panel in *Perry v. Del Rio*.[19] In November 2001 that court, in one more of the *Balderas* opinions, adopted a congressional plan for the 2002 elections. The Court plan mirrored, with three additional seats, the 1991 congressional redistricting plan. As was later pointed out by the Supreme Court, "the practical effect of this effort was to leave the 1991 Democratic Party gerrymander largely in place as a 'legal plan.'"[20]

The 2002 elections for the Texas House proved the efficacy of the DeLay strategy and the fundraising that undergirded the strategy. TAB and TRMPAC targeted 15 to 20 House races and poured in funding at unheard-of levels, with the result that Republicans took the Texas House for the first time in more than 130 years and installed Craddick as Speaker. Now the Republicans controlled both the House and Senate, and with Perry in the Governor's mansion, they could turn their attention back to congressional redistricting and fulfill DeLay's dream of remaking the Texas congressional delegation.

During the 2003 regular legislative session a new congressional redistricting plan was introduced that produced screams of outrage from Democratic forces. Finally, in frustration, unable to block the legislation, 52 House Democrats departed for Oklahoma. Known as the "Killer D's," their absence deprived the House of a quorum and blocked any further legislative action. They returned from Oklahoma only after assurances that redistricting would not be brought forward during the balance of the regular session. This ploy did not deter Governor Perry.

That summer the governor called a special session of the legislature to address redistricting. Here the battle moved to the Texas Senate, where for a time the Senate's two-thirds rule enabled Senate Democrats to block redistricting legislation. However, in a second called session the two-thirds rule was jettisoned and the redistricting legislation was moving forward when 11 Democratic senators split for Albuquerque, New Mexico. This move deprived the Senate of a quorum, again forestalling the redistricting bill. This standoff lasted a month and was broken when Senator John Whitmire returned and produced the necessary quorum. DeLay's congressional redistricting plan was enacted soon thereafter.

Prime targets of the DeLay plan were Congressmen Martin Frost of Dallas and Lloyd Doggett of Austin. Republicans failed in their run at Doggett but were successful in unseating Frost, and the 2004 congressional elections gave Republicans major victories across the state. Under the court-ordered plan of 2002, Democrats had held a 17 to 15 congressional delegation margin over Republicans; after the 2004 elections the margin had switched sides, with Republicans holding 21 congressional seats to 11 for the Democrats.

Of course, a plethora of lawsuits attacked the DeLay redistricting plan, most to no avail. Finally, in June 2006, the U.S. Supreme Court decided *LULAC v. Perry*, giving the attackers a modest victory. The Court found that the DeLay plan, in trying to save Republican Congressman Henry Bonilla, had dropped the Latino voting age population of the district from 57 percent to 46 percent (Latino voters of the district had routinely rejected Bonilla by overwhelming numbers) and thereby wrongly diluted Latino voting strength. Texas maintained its distinction of having produced at least one U.S. Supreme Court decision for every round of redistricting since 1970.

CHAPTER 4

Texas Redistricting:
A Republican Lawyer's Perspective

J. D. PAUERSTEIN

Redistricting offers opportunities to influence the composition of electoral districts for future elections and to affect the future balance of political power until the next census. In other words, redistricting is a political blood sport in which the players seek to design the field for future rounds of the electoral game. It is no surprise, then, that redistricting is hard fought, with no holds barred.

As the center of political power in Texas shifted in recent years from Democrats to Republicans, accompanied by the ascendancy of Hispanic voters and officeholders, the battles over the state's redistricting reflected the tensions between these competing groups. Their conflicting desires have repeatedly thrown redistricting to the courts, where legal battles over the composition of electoral districts have reflected the evolving face of Texas.

Modern technology has made it possible to sort voters into districts in ways that were not possible in the past. Voting districts can be tailored precisely to serve a map drawer's goals, whether political or racial. This ability has raised the stakes in redistricting by imparting a level of confidence as to future electoral outcomes that inspires map drawers and their political allies to great creativity. Predictably, the results of their legislative efforts are unacceptable to those with different goals, and so redistricting seems to inevitably end up in the courts.

The 1990s Redistricting Round

I first participated in redistricting after the 1990 census. At the time, Democrats still held the most political power in Texas, there having been little in the way of Republican political success in the state for many years. However, things were changing.

As the 1990s began, George H. W. Bush occupied the White House and Bill Clements was in his second term as governor of Texas. When the legislature took up redistricting in the 1991 legislative session, Republicans held nearly 40 percent of the seats in the House and just under 30 percent of the Senate seats.[1]

Of course, Democrats had a majority of both chambers, Ann Richards was in the governor's mansion, Bob Bullock was lieutenant governor, and Dan Morales occupied the attorney general's office. This put most of the political power pertinent to redistricting in the hands of the Democrats.

While Republicans were gaining strength, a significant change was taking place on the other side of the political spectrum. Hispanics and African Americans had long been perceived as reliable Democrat voters, but districts including them were often drawn in a manner that assured the election of Anglo Democrats. The leaning of these voters toward the Democrats was not changing, but their willingness to serve as "safe" votes for Anglo Democrats was decreasing. Instead, minority voters and the political leaders and lawyers who were aligned with them sought districts that might actually elect minority candidates, not Anglo Democrats. This trend would give rise to an interesting dynamic in redistricting as Anglo Democrats sought to hold onto power.

The 1990 census resulted in Texas gaining three new seats in the U.S. Congress. The Republicans, in light of their newly burgeoning political strength among Texas voters, thought that the districts for these seats should be drawn to correct what was seen as Republican underrepresentation in the Texas congressional delegation.

Redistricting had resulted in litigation in the 1960s, 1970s, and 1980s. Furthermore, given the political landscape, neither Republicans nor minority groups expected to be treated fairly by any legislatively adopted redistricting plans. It thus was plain that redistricting was headed for the courts once again.

In redistricting, even more than in most types of litigation, lawyers tend to think that the venue is critical to the outcome. This is a direct function of the intrinsically political nature of redistricting litigation. When law and politics collide head-on, the results are not pretty, as evidenced by redistricting. Lawyers thus seek to place redistricting before judges who they believe will lean toward their clients' political preferences; they seek to influence the outcome by winning the classic "race to the courthouse."

Early in 1991, a group that would become known as the "*Mena* Plaintiffs" filed suit against Texas in a state district court in Hidalgo County, and against U.S. Secretary of Commerce Robert Mosbacher in a federal district court in Brownsville.[2] These suits, filed in February 1991, challenged the accuracy of the 1990 census count with respect to Hispanics in south Texas. Lawyers for Republican interests were aware of these suits but were not overly concerned with them because they did not directly address redistricting.

Meanwhile, the Texas legislature was in session, and redistricting was on the agenda. The legislature passed redistricting plans for the Texas House (HB 150) and Senate (SB 31) on May 24, 1991.[3] Three days later, the legislature adjourned without adopting a congressional redistricting plan.

Although the House and Senate plans had not been signed by the governor, my law firm filed suit in federal district court on June 7, 1991. We sought to establish the forum for federal redistricting litigation by filing suit before the *Mena* plaintiffs amended their "census undercount" suits to add challenges to the redistricting plans. We chose to file in the Austin division of the United States District Court for the Western District of Texas, presided over by Judge James R. Nowlin. Judge Nowlin (a former Republican officeholder) had been appointed to the bench by President Reagan and had practiced law in San Antonio. We thus knew his background well and believed he would be preferable to most judges before whom we might try to advocate the Republican cause in redistricting.

We filed three suits, each captioned *Terrazas v. Slagle et al.*, challenging in separate cases the newly adopted House and Senate plans, and the legality of the existing congressional districts in light of the legislature's failure to craft a redistricting plan for those seats.[4] We requested a three-judge court pursuant to the Voting Rights Act, and asked that the House and Senate plans be stricken down because they diluted minority voting rights and constituted a partisan gerrymander favoring the Democrats. We also asked that the court declare the existing congressional districts unlawful in light of the 1990 census.

Ten days later, the *Mena* Plaintiffs amended their state and federal suits in south Texas to add redistricting claims. The added claims asserted generally that the legislature should not have relied on unadjusted census numbers because those numbers undercounted minority residents, particularly in south Texas, and that the House and Senate redistricting plans therefore unlawfully diluted minority voting strength. Like us, the *Mena* Plaintiffs sought to obtain a favorable forum for the redistricting litigation.

Judge Nowlin promptly requested appointment of a three-judge panel to hear our cases. On June 24, 1991, the chief judge of the Fifth Circuit appointed Circuit Judge Will Garwood and United States District Judge Walter Smith, whose federal district court was in Waco, to sit with Judge Nowlin in Austin.[5] Both were Reagan appointees, and it appeared that our decision to move quickly into court in Austin was playing out well.

Thereafter, legislative efforts to redistrict the state continued. In the second called session of the 72nd Legislature, a plan establishing new congressional districts was adopted. This plan was submitted to the Department of Justice for preclearance, as had been the state House and Senate plans. Furthermore, in late September, Texas filed a preclearance suit in the U.S. District Court for the District of Columbia, which is the statutorily mandatory venue for such a filing. This filing, I believe, was motivated by a concern that President Bush's Department of Justice would attempt to affect the redistricting litigation in Texas by delaying or denying preclearance of the state's plans.[6]

While preclearance was under consideration, Democrat and minority interests were busy trying to reach agreement on redistricting plans. These efforts focused on resolving the differences between the Anglo Democrats and the minority voting rights advocates; Republican interests were not a concern.

Eventually, lawyers for minority interests, Democrat elected officials, and Attorney General Morales reached an agreement to carve up the state as they saw fit. They then sought to use state courts in south Texas as a vehicle for imposing their agreed-upon redistricting plans on the voters of Texas. On October 7, 1991, yet another suit, *Quiroz v. Richards*, was filed in state district court in Hidalgo County.[7] This was not a truly adversarial suit; it was filed as a tool for implementing the redistricting plans that had been negotiated. *Quiroz* was filed only because the *Mena* case was stayed due to the state's appeal of an order requiring it not to use the unadjusted official census results to draw districts.[8]

The state answered the *Quiroz* suit on the very day it was filed. That same day, the *Quiroz* court entered an order approving a settlement between the plaintiffs and the state that created new districts for elections to the state Senate. As the Supreme Court of Texas explained the events leading up to this court order:

> On October 4, nineteen of the thirty-one state senators requested the Attorney General to propose an alternate senate redistricting plan to plaintiffs to settle that portion of the litigation. The Lieutenant Governor did not endorse the plan but indicated that he would abide by the will of the Senate and encouraged the Attorney General to settle the case if possible. On October 7, plaintiffs and the state defendants entered into an agreement to settle their dispute regarding state senatorial districts based upon the proposed alternate plan. In accordance with the agreement, the parties took the following actions, all on October 7, to avoid the effect of our stay of proceedings in *Mena*. Plaintiffs filed a new lawsuit against the state defendants in the 332nd District Court, styled *Quiroz v. Richards*. Plain-

tiffs alleged essentially the same claims against Senate Bill 31 as in *Mena*, but against the state defendants only. The state defendants answered. All parties filed a joint motion for entry of an agreed final judgment prohibiting any elections based upon Senate Bill 31 and ordering that elections for the State Senate be based instead on the alternate redistricting plan attached to the judgment until enactment of another under Texas law and pre-clearance under federal law. The state defendants expressly did not concede the invalidity of Senate Bill 31 and the agreed judgment did not hold the statute invalid. The district court signed the agreed judgment 'based upon the Joint Motion for Entry of Agreed Final Judgment, and arguments and stipulations of counsel.'[9]

The next day, Texas Secretary of State John Hannah submitted the "settlement plan" to the Department of Justice for preclearance. In addition, a motion to lift the stay in *Mena* was filed, and, after it was granted by the Texas Supreme Court, a "settlement plan" for the Texas House was approved by the district court in Hidalgo County on October 11, 1991.

At this point, it was plain that a Democrat Party deal blessed by sham litigation was being used as a vehicle to implement House and Senate districts entrenching Democrats.[10] As might be expected, these developments were not embraced warmly by Republicans, or by others who were not part of the deal approved in Hidalgo County.

Two state senators, Democrats Eddie Lucio of Brownsville and Bill Sims of San Angelo, sought leave to intervene in the *Mena* and *Quiroz* suits in order to reopen the litigation and attack the settlements. These efforts were opposed by all of the settling parties and rebuffed by the district court.[11]

The fact that two Democratic senators were denied leave to intervene made it clear that we would have no opportunity to be heard meaningfully in the district court in Hidalgo County. We therefore decided that extraordinary action had to be taken and brought an original mandamus proceeding in the Supreme Court of Texas. This case, *Terrazas v. Ramirez*, sought an order vacating the district court judgments establishing districts for the Texas House and Senate.[12] We also asked the court to compel Secretary of State Hannah to withdraw the *Quiroz* and *Mena* plans from preclearance consideration by the Justice Department.

At the time, five of the nine justices of the Texas Supreme Court were Democrats. However, we believed the events in the district court were sufficiently wrong that we had a reasonable chance of overturning them in that court. Our effort to do so resulted in an opinion that displayed the divisions on the supreme court to a remarkable degree. The extent to which politics would taint this case was made crystalline when Justice Bob Gammage (a Democrat and former congressman) swiveled his chair and turned his back on my partner, John McCamish, while he was arguing our side of the matter to the supreme court.

In an effort to avoid the merits of the case, our opponents argued that we should not be permitted to seek relief in the Texas Supreme Court because we had not intervened in the *Mena* and *Quiroz* cases in the district court. This argument ignored the fact that judgment was entered in the *Quiroz* case on the day it was filed, which would have made it a bit tough to intervene. It also overlooked the fact that the district court had rebuffed the efforts of Senators Sims and Lucio to intervene; if the district court turned away Democrat officeholders, it was unlikely to allow Republicans a seat at the counsel table.

A majority of the Texas Supreme Court, composed of the four Republican justices and one Democrat (Justice Raul Gonzalez), rejected the notion that we should have intervened in the district court cases and considered our application for a writ of mandamus on the merits. It held that state district courts have the authority to enter a judgment establishing a redistricting plan if the legislature fails to do so.[13] However, the court rejected the notion that a few state officials and private citizens could cut a deal to redistrict the entire state and put it into effect through an agreed judgment.[14] It therefore vacated the judgments in *Mena* and *Quiroz* and sent the cases back to the trial court.[15] This decision, which came on December 17, 1991, left the state with no effective state House or Senate redistricting plans, despite the rapidly approaching 1992 election season. The activity then shifted to the federal court.

While *Terrazas v. Ramirez* was playing out in Texas's supreme court, the federal court presiding over *Terrazas v. Slagle* held a four-day evidentiary hearing on possible interim redistricting plans for the 1992 elections.[16] This hearing was meant to put the federal court in a position to order elections under interim plans if the *Quiroz* and *Mena* settlements were vacated. Once the Supreme Court of Texas vacated the *Mena* and *Quiroz* judgments, the way was clear for action by the federal court.

The federal judges issued their opinion on December 24, 1991, leaving the legislature's congressional redistricting plan intact. However, the court ordered that the upcoming elections for the state House and Senate be held under court-ordered interim plans.[17]

These interim plans changed 30 of the 31 Senate districts and 37 of the 150 House districts.[18] In the Senate, the Republicans would gain four seats.[19] This meant the Republicans would hold 13 of the Senate's 31 seats, enough to allow them to oppose legislation by invoking the Senate's "two-thirds" rule.[20] We therefore had achieved a material outcome as to that chamber of the legislature.[21]

The court-ordered plans were not to the liking of the Democrats, of course. Governor Richards called for a special session to begin on January 2, 1992, in which the legislature adopted House and Senate redistricting plans based on the *Mena* and *Quiroz* plans. The state immediately submitted the new legislation to the Department of Justice for preclearance, and asked the federal court presiding over *Terrazas v. Slagle* to adopt these new plans on an interim basis, thereby supplanting the court-drawn plans for the March 1992 primaries.

The federal court refused to replace its plans with the legislature's newly adopted plans. Instead, it restrained the state from attempting to implement these plans for the March 1992 primaries. The state then asked the United States Supreme Court to block the elections from going forward under the court-ordered plans. The Supreme Court refused to do so, and the primaries were conducted using the districts drawn in the three-judge court's interim plans.

That was not the end of the story, however. In July 1992, the legislature's Senate redistricting plan was granted preclearance by the U.S. District Court for the District of Columbia. Secretary of State Hannah then issued a directive to election officials in which he purported to require that the general election for the Texas Senate take place under the newly precleared plan, rather than under the court-ordered plan used for the primary election.[22] This directive would have meant that candidates would stand for election in the general election in districts different from the ones that nominated them. Since all 31 Senate districts in the legislature's plan differed from those in the court-ordered plan, and many of the differences were significant, the directive divorced the nominating process from the general election.[23]

We were of the view that the general election had to be held based on the Senate districts that were used for the primary election. We also believed that Secretary of State Hannah could not validly order anything to the contrary, particularly without obtaining preclearance of his directive itself. We therefore sought relief from the three-judge court.

That court agreed with us, noting that under "common and universal usage the words 'primary elections,' with respect to offices filled by election from diverse geographically defined single member districts, mean elections in which will be chosen the party nominees for the next general election in the same district as that in which the primary election takes place." The court also held that Secretary Hannah's directive could not be implemented without undergoing preclearance. It therefore ordered that the 1992 general elections take place under its interim redistricting plans.[24]

As expected, the 1992 general election led to the election of 13 Republican senators. This change altered the dynamics of the Texas Senate. Due to the "two-thirds" rule, the Democrats had to consider the views of the Republicans and compromise with them in order to pass legislation. The redistricting litigation thus had a significant effect on Texas politics in the 1990s.

Redistricting after the 2000 Census

The 2000 census brought another round of redistricting litigation. Texas had grown in population, entitling it to two new congressional seats and increasing its delegation to 32 members. Republicans were far more dominant in state politics than they had
been in the early 1990s. No Democrat had won a statewide election since the mid-1990s, and most seats of power in state government were occupied by Republicans. Nonetheless, the gerrymandered congressional districts drawn by the Democrats in the
1990s redistricting continued to give Democrats a disproportionately high share of the congressional seats.

Under the congressional districts drawn by the Democrats in
the 1990s, the Texas congressional delegation was composed of
17 Democrats and 13 Republicans. The Republicans thus were
determined that the two new congressional seats should be drawn
to elect Republicans and that the existing congressional districts
be redrawn in a manner that would elect more Republicans. My
firm was retained to represent Congressmen Barton, Brady, Cul-
berson, DeLay, and Johnson, as well as the Republican Party of
Texas, in this effort.

Once again, the battle to establish the forum was the focus of
early events. *Terrazas v. Ramirez* had established that Texas district courts could entertain redistricting litigation. Furthermore,
the federal courts had made it clear that they would defer acting in redistricting matters until a state's legislative and judicial
branches had had ample opportunity to adopt new plans.

The Texas state courts thus would be the first to entertain
any redistricting suits. The lawyers involved in preparations for
the upcoming redistricting round accordingly began plotting to
place state court litigation in venues perceived as favorable to
their interests. This led to a race to file the first ripe lawsuit,
which would establish which state district court had primary
jurisdiction over redistricting.[25]

On December 27, 2000, before the census was released, a
group of minority voters filed *Del Rio v. Perry* in state district
court in Austin. Because the census had not been released, we

believed this filing was premature since the claims were not ripe for adjudication. We therefore did not think that this filing established the forum for the unavoidable redistricting litigation that lay ahead.

The legislature went into regular session in January 2001, and those concerned with redistricting followed its activities closely. By May 2001, the session was winding toward its end with no redistricting legislation having been passed. It therefore became increasingly likely that the courts would have to take up the task yet again.

On May 24, 2001, with the end of the regular session just a few days away, Republican interests filed suit in Houston.[26] Since it seemed clear that the legislature could not adopt redistricting plans before it adjourned, Houston was chosen as the venue for this suit because all or most of the district judges sitting there were elected as Republicans. My firm promptly intervened in this case on behalf of the Republican congressmen we represented.

A few days later, Democrat interests filed a second Travis County suit, presumably out of a concern that *Del Rio v. Perry* had been filed too early to establish jurisdiction.[27] The same day, the plaintiffs amended their pleadings in *Del Rio v. Perry* to allege that the legislature had failed to adopt redistricting plans and to request that the court do so in their stead.

On June 6, the Legislative Redistricting Board convened to consider House and Senate redistricting. Congressional redistricting is not within the LRB's jurisdiction, so the adjournment of the regular session made it likely that a state or federal court would have to draw new congressional districts. However, there was still the possibility that a special session would be called to address congressional redistricting. This meant that the pending cases might not be ripe and thus might not establish venue for all redistricting litigation.

On July 3, 2001, Governor Rick Perry informed Lieutenant Governor Bill Ratliff and House Speaker Pete Laney that he would not call a special session to consider congressional redistricting. At this point, redistricting was ripe for judicial consideration by any standard. Accordingly, on the day the governor stated he would not call a special session, a Republican filed another suit in a district court in Houston.[28] Three weeks later, the Democrats filed still another case in Austin.[29]

While all this was going on in the state courts, various parties had filed suits in the federal district courts for the Northern and Western Judicial Districts.[30] The case that ultimately would provide the forum for this cycle's federal court litigation was pending in Tyler, before Judge T. John Ward, an experienced and able federal district judge. Judge Ward had requested appointment of a three-judge court, and Fifth Circuit Judge Patrick Higginbotham and District Judge John Hannah were appointed to the panel.[31]

In July 2001, the three federal judges held that they had jurisdiction over the case, but that they were required to defer acting unless the state's redistricting processes, including state court litigation, failed to effect a timely redistricting.[32] The three-judge court set a deadline of October 1, 2001, for action by the state.[33]

Meanwhile, the parties to the state court suits continued to joust over which court—the one in Travis County or the one in Harris County—had dominant jurisdiction and would go forward with redistricting. Things came to a head when the two courts each set the redistricting cases before them for trial on September 10, 2001. It then fell to the Supreme Court of Texas to determine which court had dominant jurisdiction and would try the congressional redistricting case. The court answered that question in *Del Rio v. Perry*.[34]

The Supreme Court of Texas at the time was composed entirely of Republicans. Cynics thus felt that the outcome was foreordained and that the court in Houston would be given dominant jurisdiction. The cynics were wrong, as the Texas Supreme Court held that the court in Travis County had jurisdiction. In reaching this conclusion, the court held that redistricting litigation is not ripe until the legislature's regular session adjourns.[35] It further held that the first-filed ripe case establishes dominant jurisdiction for redistricting litigation. Here, the court held, *Cotera v. Perry*, filed immediately after the regular session ended, established jurisdiction in Travis County.[36]

This ruling was seen as a major setback by those advocating for Republican interests. It meant the case would be tried before the Honorable Paul Davis, a district judge who ran for office as a Democrat and who was perceived as a rather liberal jurist by Austin lawyers. Feeling that the Texas Supreme Court had dispatched us to serve as dinner in the lion's den, we then prepared for a trial before Judge Davis.

Judge Davis set trial for September 17, with a pretrial conference to be held on the afternoon of September 11, 2001. Needless to say, no hearing took place on September 11 due to the dark events of that day. We did, however, begin trial on September 17.

The trial lasted roughly two weeks. The Democrat interests, particularly the Democrat congressmen who intervened, argued that Judge Davis should adopt a plan that added the two new congressional districts while changing the existing map as little as possible. This was an effort to entrench the gerrymandered congressional districts drawn by the Democrats in the 1990s, despite the Republican electoral gains over the past decade. The Democrats hoped to maintain their disproportionate share of the state's congressional delegation by using the old districts as the template for most of a new map. Their lawyers therefore advanced what they claimed was a "least change" approach. In fact, however, their proposed maps would have significantly changed the districts of most Republican congressmen (not for the better) while protecting incumbent Anglo Democrats. Only the Democrats would have enjoyed the "least change" to their districts; Republicans would have been significantly disadvantaged under the Democrat plans.

For our part, the Republican interests sought adoption of maps that would have made the two new districts likely to go to a Republican candidate, and that would have undone the 1990s gerrymander. Republicans were carrying roughly 60 percent of the vote in statewide races, and we believed the composition of the state's congressional delegation should reflect that fact. We thus sought to undo the previous decade's gerrymander through plans that we believed reflected the existing political balance in the state and also advanced minority voting interests (albeit at the expense of Anglo incumbents). We hoped the latter aspect of the plan we proposed might appeal to the court and drive a wedge between the opposition parties.[37]

The trial resulted in the court's issuance of a congressional redistricting plan, Plan 1065C, on October 3, 2001. When we reviewed Plan 1065C, we were shocked to see that it was rather favorable toward Republican goals. The Democrats apparently were equally shocked, and probably dismayed, by the court's plan. Spokesmen for various Democrat groups complained vociferously in the media, decrying the court's plan. Furthermore, Speaker Laney, the *Del Rio* and *Cotera* plaintiffs, and the Democrat congressmen who had intervened in the case all filed objections to the court's plan on October 9.[38] Speaker Laney contemporaneously filed a new proposed redistricting plan.

The pressure from the Democrats apparently had the desired effect. Around 10:00 on the morning of October 10, Judge Davis sent the parties a fax in which he wrote that he was considering adopting some of Speaker Laney's proposals. Judge Davis briefly described the changes he was considering, and gave the parties until noon that day to present any objections to them. The court did not provide the parties with a map showing the changes it was considering, or any other information about them.

That afternoon, the court entered a final judgment adopting a new plan, Plan 1089C, and enjoining the state from using its existing districts for the upcoming elections. Plan 1089C was different from all of the plans that had been analyzed during the trial. Furthermore, it was far more favorable to the Democrats than the plan the court had issued just one week earlier.

Because the court's judgment included an injunction invalidating the state statute establishing the existing congressional districts, it was immediately appealable to the Supreme Court of Texas.[39] The state and all of the parties advocating for Republican interests turned to that court for relief from Judge Davis's judgment.

In the Texas Supreme Court, we asserted that Judge Davis had abridged our clients' rights under the "due course of law" provision of the Texas Constitution by imposing a plan that had not been addressed at trial, and which we had never seen before the court entered its judgment. We further argued that Judge Davis had violated the Texas Supreme Court's holding in *Terrazas v. Ramirez*, which mandated that a court cannot enter a redistricting plan without hearing evidence and allowing interested parties an opportunity to be heard. Because Plan 1089C was fashioned after the trial ended, it had not been subjected to the sort of critical analysis from counsel and expert witnesses that takes place in a redistricting trial. This, we contended, denied us the opportunity to challenge the plan and to expose any infirmities in it.

In an opinion handed down on October 19, the Texas Supreme Court overturned Judge Davis's judgment. The court found that "the manner in which the trial court entered its final judgment did not comport with *Terrazas* and violated the parties' due course of law rights."[40] As the court put it: "Once the trial court determined that it intended to substantially change its proposed redistricting plan, the constitutionally-protected interests involved, *Terrazas*, and our Constitution's due course of law provision required the trial court to provide the parties a meaningful opportunity to be heard."[41] Because Judge Davis had not afforded us such an opportunity, the court held that his judgment was "wholly invalid."[42] It then sent the case back to the trial court for retrial.

This was too much for the federal court to countenance. The three federal judges had originally set a deadline of October 1 for the state's processes to yield a congressional redistricting plan. That deadline had been extended to October 22 as the events in Austin wound on. Once Judge Davis's judgment was overturned, though, the federal court decided it had sufficiently deferred to the state's processes and that it had to act to ensure the upcoming elections could be held on schedule. Accordingly, we were able to escape from the lion's den with no redistricting plan in place.

On October 22, 2001, we began trial in a federal courtroom crowded with lawyers for the many parties to the case. This trial lasted until November 2, when the court heard closing arguments. Twelve days later, the court handed down a decision that established new congressional districts.

The court placed the two new congressional districts in Dallas and Houston, where much of the state's population growth had occurred. A number of the existing districts in Houston and Dallas could not be changed significantly because they were protected under the Voting Rights Act. The court therefore placed the new districts on the northern sides of these two cities.

The areas included in the new districts were heavily Republican. The districts went to Republican candidates in the 2002 election, after which the Texas congressional delegation consisted of 17 Democrats and 15 Republicans. We thus had achieved one of our primary goals—ensuring that the state's two new congressional districts went to Republicans. This was a step toward overcoming the Democrat gerrymander and bringing electoral outcomes more in line with the partisan composition of the state.

AUTHOR'S NOTE: The views and recollections set out in this chapter are mine alone, not those of my law firm or my clients, all of whom can speak for themselves.

CHAPTER 5

The Voting Rights Organizers

JOSÉ GARZA

The law hath not been dead, though it hath slept.
—SHAKESPEARE, "MEASURE FOR MEASURE," ACT 2, SC. 2

Meaningful participation in the Texas political process before the late 1960s was virtually closed to the Mexican American community.[1] Moreover, Mexican Americans in Texas were subjected to severe and invidious historical discrimination in housing, education, public accommodations, and politics that impaired their ability to participate in the political process.[2] The civil rights movement in the Mexican American community and numerous other factors, however, energized that community into political action in the late 1960s and early 1970s, and resulting changes slowly improved the lot of most Mexican Americans.[3] Yet, despite the success of the civil rights movement in such areas as racially segregated housing, little progress was made in increasing the number of Mexican American elected officials. For instance, in 1967, while Mexican Americans made up more than 15 percent of the Texas population, only 6 percent (9 out of 150) of the members of the Texas House of Representatives and 3 percent (1 of 31) of the Texas Senate were Mexican Americans.[4] By 1980, as the civil rights activity in Texas slowed, the number of Mexican American elected officials did not significantly increase. In 1980 the Mexican American population had increased to over 18 percent of the total, yet the number elected to the Texas House of Representatives had increased to only 15 members of the 150, or 10 percent of the total membership of the House.[5] At the local level, the picture was even more dismal. In 1973, only 72 of the 1270 (less than 6 percent) of Texas county commissioners' court members were Mexican American.[6]

Beginning in about 1979, and for several years thereafter, a litigation campaign was undertaken by three civil rights organizations. The campaign focused on using the Voting Rights Act and the one person, one vote constitutional principle to their full effect in local Texas jurisdictions. In Texas, county commissioners' courts are the governing bodies of Texas counties. They are composed of five members, four of which are elected from single-member districts commonly known as county commissioner precincts. This meant the examination of hundreds of county commissioner precincts for compliance with equal population requirements as well as racial gerrymanders involving packing or cracking Mexican American communities. The strategy also involved examination of hundreds of local at-large election systems for cities and school boards.

Voting rights jurisprudence between about 1973 and 1986 recognized the importance of historical discrimination as a factor in explaining the disparity in political participation and political power between the minority community and the Anglo community. Therefore, minority voting rights plaintiffs initially emphasized evidence of historical discrimination in their proof of vote dilution. Developing such evidence often increased the tension between the minority plaintiffs and the Anglo community. Eventually, however, the federal judiciary relegated evidence of historical discrimination to a lesser role in voting rights litigation. The evolution of vote dilution standards has more recently involved federal courts erecting a number of obstacles to minority voting rights plaintiffs' burden of proof that make political gains through court action more difficult.

History of Discrimination Evidence
in Redistricting Litigation

In 1962 the U.S. Supreme Court ended decades of refusing to enter the "political thicket" and established that reapportionment cases were justiciable.[7] Two years later, in *Reynolds v. Sims*, the Supreme Court held that the Fourteenth Amendment required state legislatures to apportion themselves by population.[8] Relying on a growing list of decisions prohibiting racial discrimination in voting under the Fifteenth Amendment, the Court in *Reynolds* found in the Fourteenth Amendment an analogous principle prohibiting the undervaluing of the voting power of individual voters.[9] The Supreme Court's ruling clearly established that "the right of suffrage can be denied by a debasement or dilution of the weight of a citizen's vote just as effectively as by wholly prohibiting the free exercise of the franchise."[10] This expansion of the Fourteenth Amendment, based on protections afforded Black citizens under the Fifteenth Amendment, provided white urban voters representation in the Alabama legislature in proportion to their numbers in the population; or, one person, one vote.[11] Thus, a plaintiff in a one person, one vote challenge was required to show nothing more than a lack of mathematical proportionality to prevail.[12]

Minority Vote Dilution

With the notion that vote dilution was actionable under the Fourteenth Amendment, minority plaintiffs filed actions challenging at-large or multimember election districts as discriminatory. Unsure of how to treat these claims, the courts initially rejected the challenges.[13]

In *White v. Regester*,[14] the Supreme Court for the first time held a multimember district unconstitutional for diluting the voting strength of racial and ethnic minorities. In sustaining the district court's findings, the Supreme Court made clear that the plaintiff's burden required more than a showing of disproportionality to its voting potential.[15] Rather, the plaintiff's burden was to establish that "the political process leading to nomination and election were [*sic*] not equally open to participation by the group in question—that members of the minority group had less opportunity than did other residents in the district to participate in the political process and to elect legislators of their choice."[16] The evidence described in *Regester* focused on the existence and effects of invidious discrimination against African Americans in Dallas and Mexican Americans in San Antonio, which resulted in unequal access to the political process.[17] Although evidence of historical discrimination against Mexican Americans and African Americans played a significant role in evaluating the claims of vote dilution, the Supreme Court failed to set any particular evidentiary standard for proving when an election system invidiously cancelled out or minimized the voting strength of minorities.

In *Zimmer v. McKeithen*,[18] the Fifth Circuit attempted to do what the Supreme Court had avoided: provide trial courts with evidentiary standards for deciding racial vote dilution cases. In *Zimmer* the court catalogued four "primary" factors and four "enhancing" factors that would prove minority vote dilution.[19] The four primary factors included showing a lack of access to the slating (recruitment and fielding) process, unresponsiveness of the legislators to the particularized needs of the minority community, a tenuous state policy for maintaining the multimember or at-large election system, and the existence of past discrimination precluding effective participation in the political process.[20] The enhancing factors were large election districts, majority vote requirement, anti–single-shot provisions,[21] and the lack of residency districts.[22] Over the next seven years the courts used the so-called *Zimmer* factors to evaluate minority vote dilution claims.[23] The *Zimmer* factors provided a fairly complex, difficult, and expensive burden of proof for minority plaintiffs challenging discriminatory election systems, but the U.S. Supreme Court in 1980 raised the bar even higher. In *City of Mobile v. Bolden*,[24] the Court ruled that a minority plaintiff's evidence must not only establish that the challenged election system resulted in discrimination, but also that it was adopted for a discriminatory purpose.[25]

In reaction to *City of Mobile*, Congress amended Section 2 of the Voting Rights Act in 1982 "to clearly establish the standards . . . for proving a violation of that section."[26] Congress intended to restore a legal standard under a "results" test by codifying the vote dilution framework embraced in *White v. Regester*.[27] Under the *Regester* framework, a plaintiff can prevail "by showing that a challenged election law or procedure, in the context of the total circumstance of the local process ha[s] the result of denying a racial or language minority an equal chance to participate in the electoral process."[28] The Senate report listed seven "typical factors" that could be probative of minority vote dilution in violation of Section 2, and two "additional factors." The seven "typical factors" were (1) historical discrimination, (2) racially polarized voting, (3) use of discriminatory voting practices, such as large election districts, majority vote requirements, and prohibitions on single-shot voting, (4) discrimination in slating, (5) socio-economic disparities between whites and minorities, (6) racial appeals in campaigns, and (7) the absence of minority representation.[29] Relegated to a less important status were the factors of lack of responsiveness and whether the challenged practice was tenuous.[30]

The Supreme Court first elaborated on the basic analytical framework established for evaluating a vote dilution claim under Section 2 in *Thornburg v. Gingles*.[31] In *Gingles* the Court provided some structure to the Section 2 standard in a case challenging North Carolina's legislative districts.[32] The Court listed the factors outlined in the Senate Report concerning the 1982 amendments to the Voting Rights Act and held:

> Under a "functional" view of the political process mandated by § 2, . . . the most important Senate Report factors bearing on § 2 challenges to multi-member districts are the "extent to which minority group members have been elected to public office in the jurisdiction" and the "extent to which voting in the elections of the state or political sub-division is racially polar-

ized" . . . If present, the other factors . . . are supportive of, but not essential to, a minority voter's claim.[33]

The Court also identified three threshold factors generally necessary to prove a Section 2 vote dilution claim:

> First, the minority group must be able to demonstrate that it is sufficiently large and geographically compact to constitute a majority in a single-member district. . . . Second, the minority group must be able to show that it is politically cohesive. . . . Third, the minority must be able to demonstrate that the white majority votes sufficiently as a bloc to enable it—in the absence of special circumstances, such as the minority candidate running unopposed . . . usually to defeat the minority's preferred candidate.[34]

Thus, *Gingles* seemed to narrow the evidentiary burden and to lessen the role of historical discrimination evidence in minority vote dilution cases brought after 1986.

Community Organizing and Texas Voting Rights Litigation

Litigation based on the 1982 amendments to Section 2 of the Voting Rights Act and the one person, one vote rule had a critical impact for Mexican American voting rights and electoral success in the 1980s and 1990s.[35] Between 1979 and 1990 the Mexican American Legal Defense and Educational Fund (MALDEF), Texas Rural Legal Aid (TRLA),[36] and Southwest Voter Registration Education Project (SVREP), together as a civil rights coalition filed scores of legal challenges against gerrymandered county commissions and at-large local jurisdictions such as cities and school boards, and were involved in statewide redistricting litigation. These legal actions were at least in part responsible for a dramatic increase in Mexican American representation at various levels of governance.[37] Although the civil rights organizations provided the resources and the lawyers, these actions would not have been possible without the courage of individual voters and activists from these communities. In the end, the lawyers and civil rights organizations could provide the resources to litigate these cases, but the individual voters, the plaintiffs, had to step forward and denounce the discriminatory obstacles to full electoral participation. Moreover, when the dust settled and the cases were over, win, lose, or draw, the lawyers retreated to their homes, while the individual plaintiffs still had to live in their communities.

Alonzo v. Jones

Evidence of historical discrimination played a vital role in the prosecution of these vote dilution cases, although to a lesser degree after *Gingles*. For example, one—and perhaps the first—minority vote dilution case in Texas, tried after the amendments to Section 2 of the Voting Rights Act, was *Alonzo v. Jones*,[38] an unreported case filed by MALDEF on behalf of Mexican American voters in Corpus Christi, Texas. The lead plaintiff in the case was Abel Alonzo. Mr. Alonzo was an outspoken community activist who had been severely injured and was confined to a wheelchair. He was instrumental in the development of the plaintiffs' case. In *Alonzo*, we submitted evidence of segregated schools, neighborhoods, and public facilities in Corpus Christi that existed until the 1960s. Moreover, plaintiffs introduced evidence of overt racial campaign appeals couched in terms of the highly controversial school busing issue. Opening these wounds was uncomfortable for all involved with the lawsuit and for the residents of the community. Additionally, Mr. Alonzo's physical condition created transportation and scheduling issues and other logistical nightmares for him. Yet no issue was more important to him than the preparation of the case, the trial itself, and the post-trial mediations. Mr. Alonzo never missed a client meeting or court hearing, and was always willing to be the public face of the legal action and the allegations of discrimination being made. In many of our cases, the community activists who came to us continued to be public spokespersons for the cause of voting equality. It was crucial to our successes that we lawyers not be the driving force, but rather that grassroots organizers continue to take a leading role with their local officials while we pushed the legal strategy.

In *Alonzo*, the district court found that the at-large election system used for city council elections in Corpus Christi violated Section 2 of the Voting Rights Act.[39] In evaluating the at-large election system the court looked at the totality of circumstances and found "historically, Mexican Americans have been the subject of discrimination throughout the State of Texas and including the City of Corpus Christi. This discrimination was pervasive, involving employment, housing, public accommodations, education, and political access. . . . Vestiges [of that discrimination] remain."[40] As a result of the decision, the City of Corpus Christi changed from a "six member, at-large, by place with majority vote" election system to a "five single-member districts and three at-large plurality vote" election system. Moreover, in the first election after implementation of the single-member district election plan, the composition of the council changed from no Mexican Americans out of six, to three Mexican Americans out of eight.

Garcia v. City of Taft

Similar results throughout Texas were achieved as a result of election plans adopted after litigation or the threat of litigation.[41] For instance, in 1983, in Taft, Texas, MALDEF, at the urging of local community activist Miguel Garcia, first threatened and then sued the city, challenging its at-large election system.

Mr. Garcia was a vibrant, muscular, former Marine. He had served his country in war and was unable to understand how Mexican Americans in Taft could be treated as if they were not equal citizens in terms of distribution of resources and the governance of the city. He constantly petitioned the city government to provide the same services on the Mexican American side of town as were provided on the Anglo side of town. Garcia urged council members to appoint Mexican Americans to boards and commissions and demanded that facilities be equally distributed to all segments of the community. He did not see any progress and decided that Mexican Americans needed to become more involved in the electoral process to prevail on these and other issues. After unsuccessful political campaigns, Mr. Garcia sought the advice of LULAC lawyers in Corpus Christi, who informed him that in their opinion, the electoral process had to change for Mexican Americans to have access to the political process. They told him that MALDEF could provide the resources and expertise to achieve that change.

Over a six- or seven-month period, Mr. Garcia journeyed often to San Antonio to urge MALDEF to help the Taft minority community in its attempts to change the local electoral process. Although MALDEF staff was sympathetic, resources simply were insufficient to allow the organization to focus on this small south Texas farming community. After all, MALDEF was engaged in statewide redistricting litigation in Arizona, New Mexico, and Texas.[42] They told him he would have to wait.

On his final visit to the San Antonio office, Mr. Garcia indicated he had convinced the city to consider and address the issue of single-member districts at the next city council meeting. He asked MALDEF to send a lawyer to help explain how single-member districts would work and how legal standards would apply to a town the size of Taft. MALDEF agreed to assist, but only in this limited role. Litigation would probably not be forthcoming.

At a hot, crowded city council meeting clearly divided along racial and ethnic lines, Mr. Garcia introduced MALDEF lawyer José Robert Juárez, telling the council it was time to change so that Mexican Americans could have an equal voice in the governance of Taft. Then Juárez explained the law and the viability of a single-member districting plan for elections in the City of Taft. He explained that with a population of about 45 percent Mexican Americans, and with an at-large election system that had produced no minority council members, not only would the litigation be expensive financially for the city, it would in all probability be successful for single-member districts.

As Juárez spoke, he was bombarded with hostile catcalls; shouts of "wetback," "trouble maker," and "go back to Mexico" came from the Anglo side of the hall. Agitated and angry at the reception he was receiving, he told the council they had an opportunity to open the process to all segments of the community and urged them to vote for that change, but if they would not, they should be advised that MALDEF was prepared to sue.

The council then entertained a motion to adopt single-member districts. There was little debate and a vote was taken. The motion failed on a 3–2 vote. After the meeting Mr. Garcia thanked MALDEF and Mr. Juárez and offered whatever assistance was necessary to begin the legal action. With the public threat of litigation having been made, MALDEF had no choice but to proceed with litigation.

Shortly after the Taft City Council rejected single-member districts, a legal action was filed pursuant to Section 2 of the Voting Rights Act, with Mr. Garcia as the lead plaintiff. MALDEF's legal action against the City began immediately with a motion for a preliminary injunction to block the impending elections. At the hearing on Plaintiffs' Motion, Mr. Garcia testified about conditions in Taft; Dr. Robert Brischetto, executive director of the Research Institute at the Southwest Voter Registration Project, testified about the existence of racial bloc voting and included evidence of the levels of discrimination against Mexican Americans in Taft; city officials were called to explain the segregated city-run facilities and lack of parks and sidewalks and drainage in the Mexican American part of town. In this small rural town just north of Corpus Christi, the plaintiffs were able to establish that the city ran a segregated cemetery deeded to the city by the Ku Klux Klan. In the city-run cemetery Anglos were buried in well-manicured grassy plots, while in a different section of the cemetery, Mexican Americans and African Americans were buried in unkempt weed-covered plots. Moreover, the neighborhoods in Taft were segregated and divided by a state highway that divided the city in half. Mexican Americans lived in a neighborhood where the streets were not curbed and open rain gutters ran in front of homes. In addition, no sidewalks or parks could be found on the Mexican American side of town. Across the highway, an Anglo neighborhood had a park with sidewalks and curbed streets. The Anglo neighborhood had concrete gutters that ran behind and between the homes. The public health clinic had separate waiting rooms, one for Anglos and one for Mexican Americans and African Americans. These conditions of separation and inequality were found to exist in Taft not just in the 1950s, 1960s, and 1970s, but even as the case was being developed in 1984. At the close of the hearing, as the trial judge took the case under advisement, the plaintiffs, including Mr. Garcia, were guardedly optimistic. They were satisfied that the lawyers and the witnesses had done their best.

The trial court, however, was not convinced. It denied the preliminary injunction because it was unconvinced the expert's analysis had determined that the racial bloc voting was not caused by some nonracial factor, such as religion or distance from the polling place, or education, or socioeconomic status. Mr. Garcia was devastated by the initial ruling, but took some comfort in the fact that he still could prevail at trial. However, as MALDEF prepared for trial, Mr. Garcia became ill. He was diagnosed with bone cancer and was scheduled for emergency surgery. He traveled to Seattle for a bone marrow transplant. As he was being taken to the operating room, he told his wife that she was to urge MALDEF to proceed with the lawsuit under any circumstance and to prosecute the case until all legal avenues were exhausted. During the operation, complications developed and Mr. Garcia did not survive the surgery. He never saw the successful conclusion of his actions.

Eventually the case settled; districts were established and two Mexican Americans were elected to the council from an election district composed of the majority Mexican American vote in a Mexican American neighborhood. As with Mr. Alonzo in Corpus Christi, Mr. Garcia's efforts in Taft led directly to changes that finally began the process for allowing the Latino community to become full partners in the American political process.

Garza v. Gonzales Independent School District

In another small south Texas community, a courageous Latina grandmother stood up and demanded the promise of our Constitution for equal and equitable political rights. Her involvement in MALDEF's litigation effort was in a lawsuit against the Gonzales Independent School District. The Gonzales ISD is a small rural school district east of San Antonio. Around 1983, Coastal Bend Legal Aid and MALDEF sued the school district, challenging the at-large election system used to elect trustees of the school board under the Voting Rights Act. Gonzales ISD's population was about 25 percent Mexican American. Yet no Mexican American had ever served on the seven-member school board. As had been found in other Texas jurisdictions, the Mexican American community in Gonzales suffered from severe segregation and discrimination. Moreover, the Mexican American community was economically dependent on the Anglo political and business establishment.

When the lawsuit was filed, the civil rights organizations represented four Mexican American businessmen and one Mexican American grandmother. However, the day after the filing, the four businessmen repudiated the lawsuit, claiming that they had never authorized the filing of any legal action, and asked that they be dismissed as plaintiffs. The grandmother, Eloisa Garza, remained steadfast on the subject that the challenge should continue. Gonzales ISD had only one polling place and had had few Mexican American candidates, and as a result, there was little statistical evidence to show racially polarized voting. The plaintiff, therefore, relied on evidence of historical discrimination and exclusion to prove her claim.

During the course of trial preparation, I met with the school district's lawyer to explore the possibility of reaching a compromise settlement. We offered the school district an election plan that would keep some at-large positions, but the majority of the trustees would be elected from single-member districts. After listening to the plaintiff's proposal, the school district's lawyer stood up from his desk, gathered up the maps that the plaintiffs' lawyers had brought in, and literally threw them out into the hall, ordering me out of his office.

The case then proceeded to trial in the U.S. District Court before the Honorable Fred Shannon of San Antonio. During the course of the trial, the plaintiff testified about the historic levels of segregation, exclusion, separate schools for Mexican American children throughout the 1960s, segregated theaters and other public facilities, and other examples of discrimination against the Mexican American community in Gonzales. The plaintiff also presented an expert witness, Dr. Fred Cervantes, who testified about his findings from official records and election returns showing that Anglos and Mexican Americans constituted separate societies. In closing arguments, I argued that the evidence, even with the paucity of election data, presented a strong case of vote dilution under the standards of the Voting Rights Act.

The defendant's counsel began his closing argument by suggesting that without stronger evidence of polarized voting, the plaintiff should be denied any relief. Almost mid-sentence, however, he paused and strayed from his prepared argument. "Judge," he said, "we cannot dispute that we do things differently in Gonzales. But you have to remember," and almost in a whisper, he continued: "we lost twelve of our boys at the Alamo." With that he closed.

The courtroom was silent for several minutes before Judge Shannon spoke. He said that normally cases of this nature would be taken under advisement and the parties allowed a period of time to present briefs on the very difficult issues that they presented. However, in this case he was prepared to rule immediately. He then stated his findings: Mexican Americans had suffered from historical discrimination that could not be denied, and the effects of that discrimination continued to the present day. In a review of the totality of the circumstances, it had become clear that the election process was not equally open to Mexican Americans. Judge Shannon also declared that the at-large election system for the Gonzales ISD violated the Voting Rights Act and the U.S. Constitution. Finally, he ordered the Gonzales ISD to develop a plan for election of school board trustees composed of seven single-member districts.

The defendants, stunned by the ruling, then approached me and said that they had dismissed their lawyer and wanted MALDEF to draw the new single-member district election plan. In the first election under the new election system, two Mexican American women were elected to the seven-member Gonzales ISD Board.

The litigation efforts of these civil rights organizations inspired by Mexican American voters also resulted in a number of "first ever" electoral successes in other areas in Texas. For instance, Medina County had not redistricted since before the turn of the century, when MALDEF and other members of the civil rights coalition sued the county under the one person, one vote principle. In the first election following a successful court challenge, the first Mexican American commissioner was elected to the county commissioners' court. In the Hondo ISD, although almost 50 percent of the population was Mexican American, no Mexican American had served on the school board until the civil rights coalition sued the school district under the Voting Rights Act. In Refugio County, only after a successful one person, one vote challenge to the county commissioner precincts was the first Mexican American elected to the county commissioners' court. In Edwards County, I was warned to get out of town before sunset as I prepared evidence and witnesses for MALDEF's one person, one vote legal challenge. Nevertheless, after MALDEF's successful legal challenge, the new majority Mexican American district elected the first Mexican American county commissioner ever to serve in Edwards County.

As mentioned previously, Mexican American representation in 1973 on the Texas county commissioners' courts was a dismal 72 of 1,270 total members (5.7 percent). After two decades of litigation and redistricting, Mexican Americans increased by

79 percent to 129 of 1,270 (10.15 percent) of the county commissioners' courts in Texas in 1994.[43] In the Texas legislature, the number of Mexican American legislators has also increased dramatically since 1980. In 1980, 15 Mexican Americans served in the Texas House of Representatives (10 percent), but this number increased to 27 in 1994 (18 percent).[44] Moreover, a study of cities that changed from at-large to some form of single-member district system suggests that the advocacy and litigation done by civil rights groups between the mid-1970s and 1990 was a substantial catalyst to a dramatic increase in representation levels for Mexican Americans.[45]

This progression toward parity would not have been possible without the courageous efforts of local voters like Mr. Alonzo, Mr. Garcia, and Ms. Garza. They have not been alone, because behind every MALDEF, SVREP, and TRLA legal action stood local voters who felt that the right to vote was worth all the scorn and scrutiny they would endure back home.

Conclusion

Underrepresentation slowly decreased between the 1970s and 1990. However, it is on the rise once again. The progress made by the Mexican American community in the past three decades is in serious jeopardy of erosion. As jurisdictions have plunged into the 2011 redistricting litigation, plaintiffs face new obstacles to successfully challenging discriminatory plans and other election practices. Judicially enacted modifications to the burden that plaintiffs must prove to successfully prevail against discriminatory electoral practices have raised yet more obstacles. For instance, in *Reyes v. City of Farmers Branch*,[46] the Fifth Circuit determined that the district court was correct in rejecting the plaintiffs' claim because the plaintiffs' evidence did not definitively establish that a single-member district in which Mexican Americans comprised over 50 percent of the citizen voting age population could be drawn. While it is true that there is nothing in this world that is certain except for death and taxes, the plaintiffs in *Reyes* had established: that the plaintiffs' proposed district contained a super majority Hispanic population of 78 percent and voting age population of about 75 percent; the contending parties (i.e., the city and the minority litigants) agreed and the district court found that because citizen voting age population was not reliable nor available at the level needed to evaluate the plaintiffs' district, Spanish surnamed voter registration data would be the most revealing; the Spanish surnamed voter registration in the plaintiffs' district was between 46.5 percent and 52.5 percent; Hispanic registered voter rates are a good measure for Hispanic citizen voting age population rates; Hispanic registered voter rates are smaller than Hispanic citizen voting age population rates; the Hispanic registered voter rate is a subset of citizen voting age population rates (eligible voter rates); and the Hispanic citizenship rate for Farmers Branch is in line with the Hispanic citizenship rate in Dallas. On these facts the district court in *Reyes* determined that it was just as likely that the district proposed by the plaintiffs was below 50 percent Hispanic citizen voting age population as it was that it was above 50 percent.

Legislators have never been shy about using minority voters to fashion districts so that the resulting plans advantage the party in power, without improvement of minority representation. The citizenship issue currently being raised in the context of redistricting, of course, disadvantages the Latino community the most. Lawsuits that have already been filed challenge the use of total population to draw our districts since total population includes non-citizens. Yet, the strength and durability of our democracy is rooted in the belief that national decisions are made by elected officials acting as representatives for all people, regardless of age, race, gender, or citizenship.[47]

In spite of the new challenges, honorable and courageous minority citizens will continue to step forward and demand their rights under our constitution. In the words of Thomas Jefferson: "In questions of power then, let no longer be heard of confidence in man but bind him down from mischief by the chains of the Constitution."

AUTHOR'S NOTE: This chapter includes discussion of cases I and other MALDEF, SVREP, TRLA, and LULAC attorneys litigated in Texas over many years. Many of these judgments were either unreported or rendered orally by a court. Thus, I discuss some of them based on my own recollection as a participant in the litigation.

CHAPTER 6

Analyzing Redistricting Outcomes

SETH C. MCKEE AND MARK J. MCKENZIE

Over the last three decades, American congressional elections have become much more competitive. Political change in Texas has been a lightning rod for its redistricting disputes, and an exemplar of the high stakes involved in this most "political" activity.[1] The Lone Star State, with its unique history as the only state ever to exist as an independent Republic, and its heroic but ultimately fatal stand at the Alamo, is not known to be timid, and its rough-and-tumble politics reflect the strong preferences of perhaps the nation's most prideful citizens.

Writing in the late 1940s in *Southern Politics in State and Nation*, V. O. Key had this to say about Texas:

> [L]ike other southern states, it is a one-party state because in 1860 a substantial part of its population consisted of Negro slaves. Most of its people then lived in East Texas, and the land to the west was largely undeveloped. The changes of nine decades have weakened the heritage of southern traditionalism, revolutionized the economy, and made Texas more western than southern. Democratic supremacy persists, although its original basis has shrunk to minor significance.[2]

Key contended that the primary fight among Democratic elites in this one-party Democratic state was over economics, with two camps—conservative and liberal—constantly battling.

Any redistribution of wealth was likely to occur under liberal leadership because this faction of the Texas Democratic Party consisted of minorities and lower-class Anglos. But with the unraveling of the New Deal coalition in the 1960s, the ranks of conservative Texas Democrats dwindled, and the faction reemerged as a remarkably homogeneous and formidable Republican opposition. Class and race are still the driving forces behind electoral politics in Texas. These two factors reinforce each other, since Anglos disproportionately reside in the upper-income brackets and align with the GOP, whereas Hispanics and especially African Americans support the Democratic Party, which is notably more liberal on economic policy and hence more responsive to the concerns of its underprivileged minority coalition.

Ironically, it was a Texas Democrat, President Lyndon Baines Johnson, who through his leadership on civil rights legislation (the 1964 Civil Rights Act and the 1965 Voting Rights Act) did more than any other politician to weaken the position of the Democratic Party in national and Texas electoral politics. He famously predicted that passage of the 1964 Civil Rights Act would result in Democrats losing the South for a generation. He was only partly right, because all subsequent generations of southerners are more supportive of the GOP than in the once hegemonic southern democracy. Since the 1960s, as Democratic dominance in Texas politics waned, Anglos reconsolidated under the Republican banner first in presidential politics and eventually in congressional elections, a pattern of Republican top-down advancement occurring throughout the American South.[3]

GOP gains in Texas U.S. House elections in the 1980s and through the 1990s would prove to be hard fought and slow-going. Thanks to their historical advantage dating back to the end of Reconstruction, an overwhelming number of Texas congressional Democrats exploited the advantages of incumbency to protect themselves from potentially viable GOP challengers. Their majorities persevered during the Reagan years and even after the 1994 "Republican Revolution" that wrested control of the U.S. House of Representatives from Democrats for the first time in forty years. Furthermore, by virtue of controlling the

Figure 6.1. The Partisan Composition of the Texas U.S. House Delegation

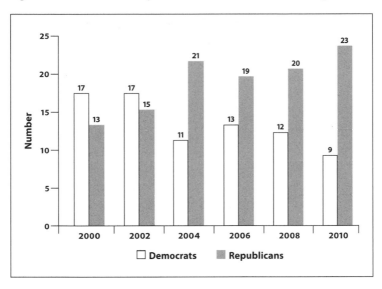

NOTE: Partisan delegation divisions are based on the results of a specific election. As noted in the text, Democrat Ralph Hall (TX 4) switched to the Republican Party before the 2004 election, making the delegation 16 Democrats and 16 Republicans.

governorship and both chambers of the legislature, Texas Democrats were in control of redrawing congressional boundaries up until Republicans took over following the 2002 elections. Indeed, the 1992 congressional redistricting plan Democrats engineered was a masterful gerrymander that served to perpetuate the party's majority for the next decade.[4]

One means to effectively limit the electoral firepower of the opposition is to pack their voters into as few districts as possible. This is what Texas Democrats did with admirable success under the congressional boundaries instated for the 1992 elections. But the Democratic gerrymander eventually succumbed to the inexorable rise of the Texas GOP. As shown in Figure 6.1, after the 2002 elections there were 17 Democrats and 15 Republicans in the Texas congressional delegation. As we will demonstrate, the 2002 court-ordered map made minimal changes to incumbents' congressional boundaries and accomplished this objective despite the addition of two congressional seats through reapportionment that were drawn to favor the GOP. Democrats were satisfied with this arrangement and indeed it was most likely the best they could hope for, since Texas Republicans were making unprecedented advances regardless of the electoral office (including a clean sweep of all statewide elective positions from 1998 to the present).

In the crucible of contemporary Texas politics, what goes around comes around. After the 2002 elections, the Texas GOP held majorities in the state House and Senate, and Republican Rick Perry easily won his first election since taking over the Governor's office when George W. Bush departed for the White House. At first it seemed nothing more than dramatic talk when rumors spread that the GOP was contemplating an unprecedented mid-decade congressional redistricting for the 2004 elections. But it soon became apparent that Texas Republicans would be relentless in pursuing their goal to redraw the congressional districts for the singular purpose of winning more seats. And in their efforts to retire certain Anglo Democratic incumbents, payback was palpable. Long-term Democratic Representative Martin Frost was a primary architect of the 1992 Democratic gerrymander, and under the 2004 Republican plan his district was carved to bits, forcing him to seek reelection against a Republican incumbent in a district comprising just 18 percent[5] of Frost's old constituency. Rather than face the inevitable, veteran Democrat Ralph Hall switched to the GOP and easily won reelection in a substantially different district than the one he had represented in 2002.

In the 2004 "re-redistricting," Republicans targeted Anglo Democrats not only to return the favor, but for obvious legal and political purposes. First, court restrictions in furtherance of Voting Rights Act provisions made it precarious to mess with large segments of voters in majority-minority districts.[6] And second, the number one complaint of Texas Republicans was the protection Anglo Democratic incumbents had cultivated in districts that were overwhelmingly supportive of the GOP in presidential contests. Some of these districts, like Democrat Charles Stenholm's 17th, were the most presidentially Republican in the entire South.[7] So when Republicans got their turn, they adopted a strategy that was the opposite of that used by the Texas Democrats, generously redistributing Anglo voters across multiple Anglo Democratic-held districts. Whereas Democrats limited GOP seats by packing Republican voters into a limited number of districts, Texas Republicans unleashed these erstwhile shoehorned constituents into those redrawn districts where Anglo Democrats sought reelection.

With devastating effect, as intended, constituencies redrawn into districts represented by Anglo Democrats were much more Republican in their voting behavior. With Anglo Democrats' old constituencies split into multiple new districts, the emergence of strong Republican challengers was anticipated. Several Anglo Democrats faced Republican opponents with the political experience and money to provide these redrawn voters with the motivation to end several long and distinguished political careers. When the dust settled from the 2004 elections, the Texas delegation contained 11 Democrats and 21 Republicans.

In 2006, Texas again redistricted (after the Supreme Court declared some of the 2003 changes to be illegal vote dilution), but this time the court-crafted changes were confined to five districts located in parts of central and south Texas (Districts 15, 21, 23, 25, and 28). The 2006 and 2008 contests were slightly more promising for Texas Democrats, in part because a strong Democratic national tide was running in both of these years. In 2006 a somewhat embarrassed, if not disgraced, Tom DeLay (District 22) left Congress, and his vacated seat was won by Democrat Nick Lampson, one of the Anglo Democratic representatives who was a casualty of the 2004 redistricting. But the 22nd district was not altered in 2006. Texas 23, represented by Hispanic Republican Henry Bonilla, was redrawn in 2006, and the removal of Anglos and infusion of Hispanic voters accounted for Bonilla's loss to former U.S. House Representative Ciro Rodriguez. Lampson's 2006 victory was erased in the next cycle, and in 2010 the electoral climate shifted strongly in favor of the GOP.

In fact, so powerful was the 2010 Republican tide that in addition to taking back District 23, Hispanic Democratic Representative Solomon Ortiz (District 27) lost,[8] and Republicans finally took out Chet Edwards (District 17), one of only two Anglo Democrats left on the Texas GOP's hit list who represented majority Anglo districts.

After the 2010 U.S. House elections, the partisan and racial composition of the Texas delegation spoke volumes about the structure of politics in a tri-ethnic state. Republicans numbered twenty-three, twenty-two of them Anglos and only one of Hispanic descent (Francisco Canseco, District 23). For a state that for most of its history only sent Anglo Democrats to Congress, of Texas's two remaining Anglo Democrats, at the time of this writing, one represents a majority Anglo District (Lloyd Doggett in District 25) and the other a majority Hispanic district (Gene Green in District 29—66.1 percent Hispanic); the other seven Democrats include four Hispanics and three African Americans.

In this chapter we provide a comprehensive account of how redistricting has affected the electoral fates of Democratic and Republican U.S. House Representatives who ran for Congress in the state of Texas from 2002 to 2010. As mentioned, parts of the Lone Star State endured back-to-back-to-back altered congressional boundaries from 2002 through 2006. Nonetheless, there were significant sections of the state where constituents experienced the effects of just a single redistricting. Overall, very few areas of the state escaped the representational dislocations associated with redrawn congressional lines. Recognizing that the electoral effects of redistricting are likely to endure beyond one election, we incorporate a unique data set that enables us to track the effects of redistricting across multiple election years—for as long as an incumbent remains in office. Our findings leave little doubt as to how electorally consequential redistricting has been for many of those fortunate enough to win a seat in the Texas congressional delegation.

The chapter proceeds in the following order. The next section details the legal wrangling over Texas redistricting in the 2000s. We follow this with an abbreviated literature review of redistricting studies related to what we do in this research. Next, we discuss our data set and methods for analyzing the effects of redistricting on incumbent vote shares. We then present our findings and conclude with a brief summary of contemporary Texas redistricting.

Court Intervention in the Political Thicket of Texas Redistricting

In some ways, the variability in constituency support for congressional incumbents in Texas during the 2000s can be traced to the seesaw nature of legislative action (or inaction) and court responses. The map changed three times over the decade—once due to the Republican legislature's mid-decade redistricting, and twice due to court-mandated redrawing of the lines. During this timeframe, the federal trial courts in Texas created a plan in 2001, affirmed the legislature's mid-decade plan in 2004, reaffirmed the same legislative plan in 2005 after the U.S. Supreme Court remanded the case for further review, and then extensively revised the south Texas portion of the legislative plan in 2006, after the U.S. Supreme Court reviewed the case a second time and changed its mind, deciding that the legislative plan was illegal after all. Consequently, there was considerable disruption of the representational relationship for numerous Texas constituencies as sections of the state's congressional boundaries were redrawn for three consecutive election cycles in 2002, 2004, and 2006. In this section, we review the legal and political circumstances surrounding the adoption of Texas's three plans over the course of the decade.

As the new decennial round of redistricting began in Texas's 2001 legislative session, Republicans controlled the state Senate by a bare majority (16 Republicans and 15 Democrats), while Democrats ran the Texas House of Representatives (78 Democrats and 72 Republicans).[9] Due to considerable population growth, reapportionment added two seats to the Texas congressional delegation, bringing the total to 32. However, Democrats and Republicans in the legislature could not agree on a new congressional map, and thus the legislative session ended with no plan for the 2002 U.S. House elections. Since states are constitutionally required by the Equal Protection Clause of the Fourteenth Amendment to redistrict every ten years to reflect population changes, the issue quickly landed in both state and federal courts. A special three-judge federal trial court convened to hear the case. It was composed of two Clinton Democratic appointees (John Hannah and T. John Ward) and one Reagan appointee (Patrick Higginbotham).[10]

In accordance with the policy of deference to state processes adopted by the U.S. Supreme Court case of *Growe v. Emison* (1993), the federal judges initially deferred to Texas state court processes to craft a plan. The Democrats had filed in state court in Travis County, a heavily Democratic county, and state district trial judge John Dietz, who oversaw the trial, was a Democrat. When the judge finally produced a plan, some Republicans perceived the plan as overly favorable to Democrats. Though the federal court had already extended the deadline given to the state court, it provided additional time for the Republicans to appeal to the state supreme court. The Republican-controlled state supreme court vacated the Democratic trial judge's plan, leaving the task of producing the congressional map to the three federal judges.[11]

Following the advice of Rice University political scientist John Alford, the federal judges drew the two new congressional districts in the geographic areas that saw the most population growth (in north Dallas and central Texas). Map 6.1 shows the congressional boundaries for the 2000 elections with Democratic districts in white and Republican districts in gray. Map 6.2 shows the altered lines based on the 2001 redistricting ordered by the three-judge federal court. Although the court claimed they did not use old district lines as independent locators to fill out the rest of the map, the similarities between the 2000 and 2002 maps are quite apparent, with the main exceptions relating to the insertions of the new District 31 between Houston and Austin and the new District 32 in Dallas. Essentially, the court left the 1991

Map 6.1. Texas Congressional Districts after the 2000 Elections

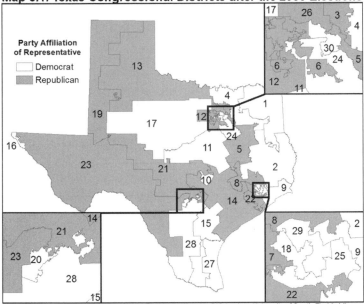

Map created by Richard McKenzie, GIS Analyst, University of South Florida Library.

Democratic gerrymander in place.[12] This fact was evidenced by the 2002 election results, where Democrats continued to maintain a 17–15 lead in the number of congressional seats held, despite Republicans receiving 55 percent of the overall U.S. House vote in the state.[13]

After the 2002 elections, Republicans captured the Texas House of Representatives, giving them control of all three branches of state government for the first time since Reconstruction. At the urging of then-U.S. House Majority Leader Tom DeLay and other Republicans, the state GOP leadership in the 2003 legislative session attempted to redraw the congressional districts for naked partisan gain.[14] The first attempt failed, as most Democratic state representatives fled to Ardmore, Oklahoma, in order to deny Republicans an operating quorum. After the regular legislative session ended, Republican Governor Rick Perry called a special session, but this time Democratic state senators fled to New Mexico, again denying Republicans the

Map 6.2. Texas Congressional Districts after the 2002 Elections

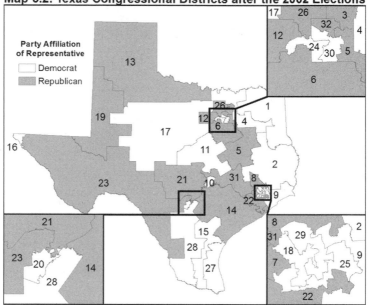

Map created by Richard McKenzie, GIS Analyst, University of South Florida Library.

quorum they needed to conduct business. Governor Perry called two more special sessions before Republicans were able to muscle their plan through. In this plan, Republicans used the opportunity to shore up the electoral position of Republican Congressman Henry Bonilla, of San Antonio, by cutting the border city of Laredo in half and shedding thousands of Hispanic voters from Bonilla's District 23, shifting them over to District 28. Bonilla had been steadily losing support among the Hispanic community in successive elections, and the easiest way to stop the slide in support was to cast out many Hispanic voters from Bonilla's district. This action, however, decreased by one the number of majority Hispanic districts in the state in terms of citizen voting age population.

To make up for this loss of majority Hispanic districts, Republicans radically altered District 25, connecting Hispanic voters in Austin with Hispanic voters way down in the Rio Grande Valley—300 miles to the south. Republicans also used this re-

Map 6.3. Texas Congressional Districts after the 2004 Elections

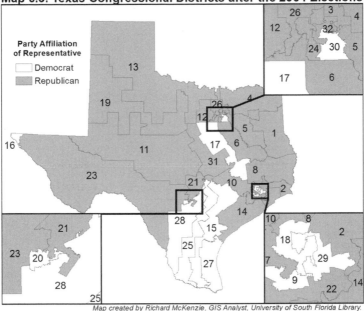

Map created by Richard McKenzie, GIS Analyst, University of South Florida Library.

redistricting opportunity to alter many of the district boundaries around the state, with the objective being to redistribute
voters into Anglo Democrat districts, thereby upsetting the incumbency advantage that these representatives enjoyed. Map 6.3
presents the Republican partisan gerrymander. Contrasted with
Map 6.2, the shading on this map provides a nice illustration of
the significant number of Democrats who were defeated in the
2004 elections.

Almost immediately after the Republican congressional plan
was adopted, the League of United Latin American Citizens
(LULAC) and other groups challenged its legality in federal
court. Specifically, LULAC and others argued that the plan constituted a violation of the Voting Rights Act and that it was an
unconstitutional racial gerrymander, an unconstitutional mid-
decade redistricting, and an unconstitutional partisan gerrymander. The composition of the new three-judge federal court
was similar to the 2001 court, except this time Republican ap-

pointee Lee Rosenthal sat on the panel instead of Democrat John Hannah. Thus, unlike the 2001 federal court, Republican appointees dominated this federal court.

Not surprisingly, when the federal court issued its ruling in *Session v. Perry*, in January 2004, the two Republican judges upheld the validity of the Republican state legislature's redistricting plan while lone Democrat T. John Ward dissented from the decision. One cannot rule out the possibility of some partisan favoritism (i.e., federal judges deciding a certain way simply to help out their own party), but this is not to say that the partisan predisposition of the judges was the only factor in their decision.[15] One could also argue that these judges had very principled differences regarding their own ideological conceptions of the law. In fact, Judge Ward agreed with most of the legal reasoning of the two Republican judges, concurring with their decision to dismiss most of the claims involving the VRA as well as other claims of unconstitutional mid-decade redistricting, partisan gerrymandering, and racial gerrymandering.

Where Judge Ward parted with his colleagues was in the legality of splitting up the city of Laredo (Webb County), located in Congressman Bonilla's District 23. The U.S. Supreme Court later agreed with and essentially adopted Ward's reasoning. The Voting Rights Act is frequently employed as a weapon in legal challenges to redistricting plans, as José Garza discusses in Chapter 5, and the legal precedent and structure behind these challenges can sometimes appear deceptively straightforward; but in practical terms, the VRA's application to redistricting is unclear and inconsistently applied by courts.[16] The U.S. Supreme Court appeared to offer somewhat brightline rules for VRA challenges to redistricting in *Thornburg v. Gingles* (1986).[17] The three-prong threshold test calls for a court to consider (1) whether a minority group is sufficiently large in number to constitute a majority in a relatively compact district, (2) whether the minority group is politically cohesive, and (3) whether the white majority always votes in a way to defeat the preferred candidate of the minority group. Finally, courts must consider a "totality of the circumstances" test, which includes a number of factors that a judge can then use to claim evidence of VRA violations.

A series of VRA cases issued by the Supreme Court and lower courts since the *Gingles* case have not offered clear legal guidance. The result of the confusing and ambiguous line of cases that follow the VRA statute is that judges' ideological or partisan views heavily influence their interpretations of VRA precedent.[18]

Judge Ward argued that the state legislature could not simply make up for the loss of a Hispanic citizen voting age population majority district by creating another Hispanic majority district connecting disparate and geographically distant Hispanic populations in central Austin and the Rio Grande Valley. In fact, such a noncompact district as 25 would not even be required under the court-interpreted provisions of the Voting Rights Act.[19] On the other hand, Ward believed that the splitting of Laredo violated the VRA because the Hispanic population was sufficiently large to constitute its own district when coupled with nearby Hispanic populations, evidence of racial bloc voting existed, and Hispanic voters' preferred candidates were losing to Representative Bonilla.[20]

The plaintiffs appealed to the U.S Supreme Court, where the Court vacated the lower court decision of *Session v. Perry* and then remanded the case back to the lower court, presumably to give the lower court judges the chance to consider their ruling in light of the Supreme Court's partisan gerrymandering case *Vieth v. Jubelirer* (2004). The cryptic language of the high court presumably circumscribed the three-judge lower court's review solely to questions of partisan gerrymandering.[21] The elections of 2004 then proceeded under the map drawn by the Republican legislature. In 2005, the three-judge federal court finished its review of the case, and all three judges came to the conclusion that the Republican plan did not rise to the level of an unconstitutional partisan gerrymander.[22]

Again plaintiffs appealed, and again the U.S. Supreme Court considered the merits of the case. This time, before the 2006 elections, the U.S. Supreme Court issued its decision in *LULAC v. Perry* (2006), striking down parts of the Republican plan in south Texas as constituting violations of Section 2 of the VRA. The court majority was concerned with joining two Hispanic communities as far away as Austin (in central Texas) and McAllen (near the border with Mexico) in order to swap out the loss of a majority Hispanic citizen voting age district in Bonilla's District 23. The three *Gingles* factors for creating a Hispanic majority district in 23 were present, and using District 25 to make up for that district was not adequate, said the Court.[23] Furthermore, in the "totality of the circumstances" test, the Court found additional evidence that the racial effect on Hispanic voters was significant. According to Kennedy in his majority opinion, "Even assuming Plan 1374C provides something close to proportional representation for Latinos, its troubling blend of politics and race—and the resulting vote dilution of a group that was beginning to achieve §2's goal of overcoming prior electoral discrimination—cannot be sustained."[24] The Supreme Court dismissed the VRA claims brought by African American groups.

On remand in August 2006, the three-judge district court issued the opinion of *LULAC v. Perry*,[25] recombining Webb County (Laredo) into District 28 and compressing the bacon-strip (sometimes referred to as fajita-strip) District 25 of incumbent Democrat Lloyd Doggett to make it more of an Austin-based district again—though the center of Austin was still left split among several districts. Bonilla's District 23 was then given more Hispanic voters from Bexar County. In partial exchange, Bonilla's district gave up the more Republican-leaning counties of the west Texas German Hill Country to Lamar Smith's District 21 (these included such counties as Kerr and Kendall, classic Republican strongholds of German descent dating back to the Civil War). In the subsequent election a few months later, in the midst of an election year favoring Democratic candidates, and with an increased Hispanic population, the new voters and added Hispanic vote were factors sufficient to deny Bonilla another election victory. Map 6.4 is a depiction of the federal court map of 2006 as it looked after election results in 2010, representing these changes in the south Texas districts.

Though the initial federal court map of 2006 resulted in Republicans losing Bonilla's seat in District 23, as one can see in Map 6.4 the loss of that Hispanic majority district had been reversed in the wake of the 2010 Republican wave election. In that year,

Map 6.4. Texas Congressional Districts after the 2010 Elections

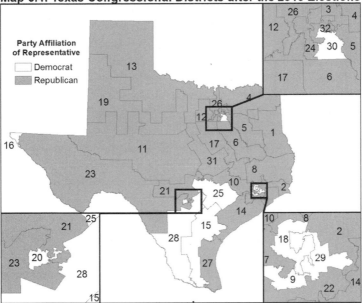

Map created by Richard McKenzie, GIS Analyst, University of South Florida Library.

Republicans even picked up the Hispanic majority District 27 (a district that was altered by Republicans in 2004 but left alone by the 2006 federal court) by a razor-thin margin, in part due to lingering redrawn voters from the 2004 Republican gerrymander who remained in the district as of 2010 but provided Democratic Congressman Solomon Ortiz with less support when compared to other voters—a situation we detail shortly.

Redistricting and Voter Preferences

Redistricting strikes at the core of representation because it alters the relationship between voter and representative. For most incumbents it takes time, sometimes years, to nurture a relationship with their voters that goes beyond mere name recognition. All incumbents cultivate a certain "home style" or means of presenting themselves to their constituents.[26] And the effort invested in getting to know their voters on a more personal level can yield considerable electoral dividends. Indeed, by fostering a personal vote as opposed to a partisan vote, there are incumbents who win reelection only because a segment of the electorate crosses partisan lines to vote for them.[27] This is apparent based on indicators like district partisanship, in which the two-party presidential vote clearly favors the party opposite that of the district incumbent. From the 1960s through the 1980s a good number of these so-called "split results" districts gave a majority of presidential votes to the GOP and a majority of House votes to the Democrat.[28]

In the 1990s, Anglo Democrats in Texas stood out by constituting a group of incumbents who relied heavily on the personal vote in order to win reelection in presidentially Republican districts. Maximizing the incumbency advantage in terms of promoting name recognition and then taking it a step further by receiving high marks for service-related work proved to be the path to victory for so many of these southern Democratic representatives who, based on district partisanship, should not have been reelected.[29] Texas Republicans recognized that, given such a disparity between the decidedly Republican district-based presidential vote and the fact that most of these Anglo Democrats managed to win another term, another redistricting would be the perfect remedy for ending this electoral imbalance.

The simple act of redrawing congressional boundaries has the potential to dramatically alter the partisan outcome of U.S. House elections. First, an immediate effect of redistricting on political behavior is a decline in voter familiarity with the incumbent. Specifically, voters who have a different incumbent running for reelection in their district as a consequence of redistricting— those we refer to as redrawn constituents—are significantly less likely to recall or recognize the name of their new incumbent.[30] Second, as a result of their lower likelihood of knowing who in fact is their incumbent, redrawn voters are more susceptible to the appeals of challengers.[31] In sum, the incumbency advantage, which these vulnerable incumbents have taken years to develop, is null and void in the case of most redrawn constituents.

To make matters worse for incumbents representing greatly altered districts containing a large number of redrawn voters, this predicament attracts the attention of strong challengers. Because so many constituents are essentially new to the incumbent, challengers know that those voters are up for grabs.[32] It is no surprise then that challengers raise more money in districts that contain a higher percentage of redrawn constituents,[33] stronger challengers emerge in districts with more redrawn constituents,[34] and the number of high-quality challengers is greatest in redistricting years.[35]

There remains one final variable to consider when assessing the role of redistricting on voter preferences: the political situation at the time a redistricting is implemented. Because redrawn constituents lack a bond with the incumbent seeking reelection in their district, the short-term political situation will have a greater influence on these voters' candidate preferences vis-à-vis the preferences of voters who retain the same incumbent after redistricting.[36] *Ceteris paribus*, because of their cultivation of a personal vote, when the electorate turns against the party of the incumbent, they will retain more support from those voters they represented before redistricting.[37] By contrast, redrawn voters are much more likely to shift their votes in favor of the partisan tide, and if the party benefiting from short-term conditions is that of the challenger, then redrawn voters can be the linchpin for defeating the incumbent.

Previous research has demonstrated with district-level and individual-level data in those years that clearly broke in favor of one party, redrawn constituents were more supportive of candidates affiliated with the party advantaged by short-term and long-term conditions.[38] Furthermore, in the South, where political conditions in the 1990s and the early part of the 2000s (2002 and 2004) favored the GOP, the white electorate continued to realign in favor of the Republican Party, accentuating the partisan effects of redistricting[39] and disproportionately reducing the number of votes garnered by Anglo Democratic incumbents.

By altering the representational relationship between voter and representative, and considering the effect this has on constituent political behavior, it is evident just how electorally disruptive a redistricting can be. As we mentioned previously, Texas Democrats proved deft in their ability to craft a map that minimized Republican gains in the 1990s redistricting round. And for the initial congressional plan enacted for the 2002 elections, minimal district alterations ensured minor electoral effects. But 2004 broke with precedent because a mid-decade plan was instated that drastically altered congressional boundaries with the specific intent of overloading the districts of Anglo Democratic representatives with redrawn constituents. Hence, it was not about simply making sure Anglo Democrats represented heavily Republican constituencies, since most already did. Instead, it was about disrupting the representational relationship[40] by redistributing the lion's share of redrawn voters to Democratic incumbents because redrawn constituents' existing proclivity to vote Republican would be further reinforced by the emergence of strong Republican challengers and favorable short-term conditions (including a Texan Republican President running for re-election). Under this scenario it is no wonder that the Texas Republican redistricting strategy in 2004 was a glowing success.

Nonetheless, the next two election cycles (2006 and 2008) bent in favor of the Democratic Party, and in 2006 a partial redistricting of the state clearly benefited Democrats, who defeated Hispanic Republican Henry Bonilla (District 23). But by the time 2010 rolled around, the last election under the congressional boundaries valid since 2006, short-term conditions broke decisively in favor of Republicans and the party bested their previous high watermark of 2004.

Voter preferences have been affected by the circumstances surrounding boundary changes, and consequently Texas redistricting in the 2000s has shown notable variability in its effects on U.S. House elections. We do not, however, assume that the effects of redistricting last for only one election cycle. Therefore, we are interested not just in how incumbent vote shares are altered by the presence of redrawn voters immediately after redistricting, but also how well incumbents fare in subsequent elections according to the length of time they have represented a particular group of constituents. In the next section we explain the data we have used to determine the effects of redistricting on the vote shares of Democratic and Republican congressional incumbents who won election between 2002 and 2010.

Data and Methods

The data for our descriptive and multivariate analyses were provided by the Texas Legislative Council (TLC).[41] In order to assess the effects of redistricting on incumbent vote shares, the unit of analysis we rely on is the Voting Tabulation District (VTD). Although not exactly equivalent, a VTD is similar to a precinct because it is the smallest aggregate unit for vote returns. In Texas, VTDs are the geographic building blocks used to aggregate up to the congressional district. The TLC created VTDs in order to join U.S. Census population data (i.e., the total number of African Americans, Hispanics, and Anglos) with precinct-level election returns.[42]

For the 2010 elections the TLC created 8,400 general election VTDs. Fortunately for us, and what we consider to be an advancement in the study of redistricting, the TLC reformatted both its election returns and population data to align with the 2010 VTDs. Election returns from 1996 to 2010 are now reported based on the configuration of the 2010 VTDs. Likewise, 2000 census population data, including totals and racial composition, are arranged according to the 2010 VTDs. Standardizing population and election data on one set of VTDs allows us to evaluate the influence of redistricting on incumbent vote shares from the first redistricting of interest, 2002, up through the 2010 Texas U.S. House elections.

The VTD data do not come with an indicator for the corresponding congressional district. In order to match each VTD with the correct congressional district for each election from 2002 to 2010, we had to use Geographic Information Systems (GIS) software. With GIS we were able to overlay each Texas congressional map[43] onto the 2010 VTD map and then create a new variable for the congressional district number corresponding to each VTD. We performed this operation on a VTD map that contained U.S. Census population data. Once we added all of the relevant congressional district numbers to the VTD map that includes population data, we then joined these data with the VTD-level data containing all of the congressional election returns from 2002 through 2010. Thus at the VTD level, we have collected data on U.S. House votes and the Voting Age Population (VAP). In addition to the total VAP in each VTD, we also have the total VAP for Anglos (AVAP), Blacks (BVAP), Hispanics (HVAP), and Others (OVAP).

With the inclusion of a congressional district indicator for each VTD, we are able to determine which VTDs have migrated from one incumbent to another from 2002 to 2010. This determination is the key to our analysis of the effects of redistricting on incumbent vote shares. Recall that Texas redrew its congressional boundaries in three consecutive elections: 2002, 2004, and 2006. Whereas the 2002 and 2004 changes affected all congressional districts, the 2006 redistricting only altered the boundaries in Districts 15, 21, 23, 25, and 28. By examining the congressional district number assigned to each VTD for each election, we can classify VTDs as open, same, or redrawn for a given election year. And since 2006 was the last time congressional districts were reconfigured, it follows that all VTDs remained with the same incumbent from 2006 to 2010.[44]

For any given election, a VTD is designated as open if it resides in a congressional district that does not contain an incumbent seeking reelection. We exclude all open-seat VTDs/districts from our analysis.[45] A VTD is defined as "same" if it remained with the same incumbent before and after a redistricting. For instance, in 2002 Democrat Lloyd Doggett represented District 10; in 2004 his district was substantially altered, making it a Republican bastion. Doggett chose to seek reelection in the redrawn District 25, which contained some sections of his old district from 2002 (constituents who resided in southeast Austin). Those VTDs designated as part of District 10 in 2002 and assigned to District 25 in 2004 constituted Doggett's same VTDs for the 2004 election.

Finally, a VTD is redrawn if redistricting moves it from one incumbent to another. Again we will use Democratic Representative Lloyd Doggett as an example to explain what we mean by a redrawn VTD. First, in 2002, Doggett's District 10 was overpopulated. Redistricting, instead of altering the district by swapping different areas in and out, simply downsized it. Thus Doggett retained the same constituents he represented before the 2002 redistricting, while the rest of his constituents were placed in neighboring districts. By contrast, District 25, where Doggett ran for reelection in 2004, contained 66,268 constituents (10.2 percent of the entire district population) who were represented by Republican Congressman Ron Paul (District 14) in 2002.[46] Therefore, all of the VTDs that were in District 14 in 2002 and then placed in District 25 in 2004 are defined as redrawn for the 2004 election.

Sticking with the case of Congressman Doggett, the analysis is further refined because his district was once again substantially altered in 2006. For the 2006 boundaries in District 25, there were 191,337 constituents (29.4 percent of the entire district population) who were represented by Republican Congressman Lamar Smith (District 21) in 2004. Hence, all of the VTDs that were in District 21 in 2004 and then placed in District 25 in 2006 are defined as redrawn for the 2006 election.

It is necessary to explain this progression of VTD swapping in consecutive redistrictings for a single incumbent because it highlights how we classify VTDs.[47] Furthermore, it shows how we can assess potential differences in an incumbent's vote shares according to when the VTDs were drawn into the representative's district. So, in the case of Congressman Doggett, by the time we arrived at the 2006 election his district consisted of three different categories of VTDs: (1) the VTDs he had retained since the 2000 election, (2) the VTDs he had retained since 2004 (those redrawn in 2004), and (3) the VTDs drawn into his district in 2006.

Given these three distinct categories of VTDs for Congressman Doggett, which are distinguished by the election year in which he inherited them, it is evident that if we proceed to 2008 and 2010, then the VTDs are now classified as: (1) the VTDs he retained since the 2000 election, (2) the VTDs he retained since 2004 (those redrawn in 2004), and (3) the VTDs he retained since 2006 (those redrawn in 2006). Because we are working with the same exact VTDs for all of the elections we analyze, we can correctly classify all VTDs for every incumbent who sought re-election from 2002 to 2010. So if an incumbent draws a major party challenger (a Republican or Democrat), then for this specific election, say 2002, we can determine their share of the two-party vote according to each VTD category relevant to their district (e.g., redrawn VTDs in 2002 and same VTDs since 2000).

This type of analysis enables us to assess the level of support an incumbent receives based on the length of time he has represented a certain segment of constituents.[48] In other words, we can determine how redistricting affects incumbent vote shares across multiple elections—for as long as an incumbent retains his or her seat. We put this method to use in the following sections of the chapter, with descriptive and multivariate analyses, respectively.

Redrawn Constituents

Before turning to the analysis of vote shares for Democratic and Republican incumbents, we begin this section by displaying the voting age percentage of redrawn constituents each representative inherited in 2002, 2004, and 2006. In Table 6.1[49] the contrast between the 2002 and 2004 redistrictings is stark. Boundary changes in 2002 were fairly minimal. Whereas the average percentage of redrawn constituents was 18 percent for incumbents of both parties in 2002 (10 percent for Democrats and 28 percent for Republicans), in 2004 the average redrawn percentage of constituents was 41 percent (45 percent for Democrats and 38 percent for Republicans). And with the exception of Republican Pete Sessions, who left District 5 in 2002 and moved into the new District 32, where 85 percent of his constituents were new to him, no other incumbent in 2002 had a district in which a majority of the VAP was new to them.

Table 6.1. The Voting Age Percentage of Redrawn Constituents for Democratic and Republican Incumbents

Democrats	2002	2004	2006	Republicans	2002	2004	2006
Max Sandlin (1)	11	61	—	Sam Johnson (3)	11	18	—
Jim Turner (2)	7	—	—	Ralph Hall (4)	—	66	—
Ralph Hall (4)	10	—	—	Jeb Hensarling (5)	—	39	—
Nick Lampson (9, 2)	3	54	—	Joe Barton (6)	49	28	—
Lloyd Doggett (10, 25)	0	61	58	John Culberson (7)	22	50	—
Chet Edwards (11, 17)	10	67	—	Kevin Brady (8)	13	53	—
Ruben Hinojosa (15)	4	39	15	Kay Granger (12)	42	17	—
Silvestre Reyes (16)	9	0	—	Mac Thornberry (13)	29	12	—
Charles Stenholm (17, 19)	12	70	—	Ron Paul (14)	27	63	—
Sheila Jackson Lee (18)	8	25	—	Randy Neugebauer (19)	—	41	—
Charles Gonzales (20)	4	14	—	Lamar Smith (21)	37	33	28
Martin Frost (24, 32)	32	82	—	Tom DeLay (22)	8	25	—
Solomon Ortiz (27)	3	12	—	Henry Bonilla (23)	1	17	31
Ciro Rodriguez (28)	20	—	—	Michael Burgess (26)	—	42	—
Henry Cuellar (28)	—	—	53	John Carter (31)	—	62	—
Gene Green (29)	0	22	—	Pete Sessions (32)	85	45	—
Eddie Bernice Johnson (30)	11	25	—				
Democrats and Republicans	18	41	37				
Democrats	10	45	43	Republicans	28	38	29
Anglo Democrats	12	60	58				
Minority Democrats	8	19	35				

Note: Data provided by the Texas Legislative Council. Data on the voting age population (VAP) were provided at the Voting Tabulation District (VTD) level and were aggregated up to the congressional district. The redrawn VAP percentage is the district portion of persons 18 or older the incumbent inherited as a consequence of redistricting. For instance, in 2002 in District 1, Democratic incumbent Max Sandlin's voting age population was 527,366 and the number of redrawn voting age residents was 56,061; therefore the redrawn voting age percentage of constituents is 11 percent (56,061/527,366).

By comparison, in 2004 there were five Republicans and six Democrats who sought reelection in districts reconfigured to contain half or more redrawn voting age residents. Under this GOP-drawn map, none of these Republicans were placed in electoral peril by the addition of so many redrawn voters, but most of these Democrats with more than half of their voting electorate consisting of redrawn constituents were. It is no surprise that all of these Democratic incumbents were Anglos targeted for defeat; as mentioned previously, the strategy was to overload their districts with redrawn voters. Excluding Gene Green—who, representing majority Hispanic District 29, was the only Anglo Democrat not in the GOP's crosshairs, and who had a district with relatively minor changes (just 22 percent redrawn in 2004)—the six Anglo Democrats (Sandlin, Lampson, Doggett, Edwards, Stenholm, and Frost) that Texas Republicans aimed to defeat ran in districts where the average percentage of redrawn voting age constituents was 65 percent. To make matters even worse, Democrats Charles Stenholm and Martin Frost sought reelection in districts with Republican incumbents (Randy Neugebauer in District 19 and Pete Sessions in District 32) who retained a much greater share of their constituents from the 2002 redistricting.

In 2004, all of the Republican incumbents won reelection.[50] Among Anglo Democrats, Jim Turner chose retirement, Ralph Hall switched parties and easily won another term as a Republican in a district where two-thirds of his VAP was redrawn, and Lloyd Doggett cruised to reelection in the vastly reconfigured majority Hispanic District 25. Chet Edwards once again displayed his remarkable resilience by winning reelection in a greatly altered and presidentially Republican District 17.[51] Max Sandlin and Nick Lampson both lost to quality Republican challengers and Charles Stenholm and Martin Frost succumbed to Republican Congressmen Randy Neugebauer and Pete Sessions, respectively. As intended, and made evident by their much lower percentages of redrawn constituents (an average of 19 percent), none of the minority Democrats who made it to the general election[52] were in danger of losing.

In the 2006 elections, all but five districts remained unchanged since 2004. The geographically isolated redistricting of 2006 altered the congressional boundaries of Anglo Democrat Lloyd Doggett (58 percent redrawn), Hispanic Democrats Ruben Hinojosa (15 percent redrawn) and Henry Cuellar (53 percent redrawn), Anglo Republican Lamar Smith (28 percent redrawn), and Hispanic Republican Henry Bonilla (31 percent redrawn). The immediate effect of these redrawn lines was the defeat of Republican Henry Bonilla by former Democratic Congressman Ciro Rodriguez. Although it is apparent that redistricting was directly responsible for Bonilla's loss in 2006, the effects of redistricting can linger for several elections, and we will show this in the analyses that follow.

Redistricting and Incumbent Vote Shares

Table 6.2 presents all of the Democratic and Republican incumbents included in our vote share analysis. As stated in the note below Table 6.2, this constitutes the entirety of Texas U.S. House incumbents whose districts were altered at least once, who sought reelection, and who faced a major party opponent sometime between the 2002 and 2010 elections. We provide checkmarks to denote the election year in which an incumbent's vote share is shown in the descriptive results. We do not include checkmarks in the case of an open-seat election, an uncontested election, or elections in which the incumbent was no longer running because they were defeated or retired. For example, there is no checkmark for Republican Sam Johnson in 2004 because he did not face a Democratic challenger. There is no checkmark for Republican Michael Burgess in 2002 because he was not an incumbent at the time of this election—he won District 26 in 2002 when it opened up with the departure of Republican Congressman Dick Armey. As for incumbents who were defeated (Bonilla in 2006) or retired (Turner in 2004 and DeLay in 2006), there are obviously no more checkmarks for them for the years after they leave.

In the next two tables we display the vote shares of Demo-

Table 6.2. Democratic and Republican Incumbents Included in Redistricting Analyses

Democrats	2002	2004	2006	2008	2010	Republicans	2002	2004	2006	2008	2010
Max Sandlin (1)	✓	✓				Sam Johnson (3)	✓		✓	✓	✓
Jim Turner (2)	✓					Ralph Hall (4)		✓	✓	✓	✓
Ralph Hall (4)	✓					Jeb Hensarling (5)		✓	✓		✓
Nick Lampson (9, 2)	✓	✓				Joe Barton (6)	✓		✓	✓	✓
Lloyd Doggett (10, 25)		✓	✓	✓	✓	John Culberson (7)		✓	✓	✓	
Chet Edwards (11, 17)	✓	✓	✓	✓	✓	Kevin Brady (8)		✓	✓	✓	✓
Ruben Hinojosa (15)		✓	✓	✓	✓	Kay Granger (12)		✓	✓	✓	✓
Silvestre Reyes (16)		✓		✓	✓	Mac Thornberry (13)	✓	✓	✓	✓	
Charles Stenholm (17, 19)	✓	✓				Ron Paul (14)	✓		✓		✓
Sheila Jackson Lee (18)	✓		✓	✓	✓	Randy Neugebauer (19)		✓	✓	✓	✓
Charles Gonzales (20)		✓		✓	✓	Lamar Smith (21)	✓	✓	✓		
Martin Frost (24, 32)	✓	✓				Tom DeLay (22)	✓	✓			
Solomon Ortiz (27)	✓	✓	✓	✓	✓	Henry Bonilla (23)	✓	✓	✓		
Ciro Rodriguez (28)	✓				✓	Michael Burgess (26)		✓	✓	✓	✓
Henry Cuellar (28)			✓	✓	✓	John Carter (31)		✓	✓	✓	✓
Gene Green (29)			✓	✓	✓	Pete Sessions (32)	✓	✓	✓	✓	✓
Eddie Bernice Johnson (30)	✓										
N	11	10	7	9	10	N	8	13	15	11	11

Note: This constitutes the entirety of Texas U.S. House incumbents whose districts were altered at least once, who sought reelection, and who faced a major party opponent sometime between the 2002 and 2010 elections. Democrats Nick Lampson, Lloyd Doggett, Chet Edwards, Charles Stenholm, and Martin Frost each ran in districts with a different number between the 2002 and 2004 elections.

cratic and Republican incumbents, respectively, for all of the requisite elections according to the checkmarks displayed in Table 6.2. The first table shows the two-party vote Democratic incumbents received, and the second table presents the two-party vote won by Republican incumbents. These vote returns highlight the strong contrast in the partisan effects of Texas congressional redistricting from 2002 through 2010. The presence of redrawn VTDs wreaked havoc on the reelection bids of several Democrats, but only ended the political career of a single Republican incumbent.

Table 6.3 displays the two-party vote for Democratic incumbents classified according to when a segment of VTDs were received by each representative. An "S" means that this portion of the vote comes from constituents whom the incumbent has represented since 2000 (or even earlier) or since the first election in which the representative ran as an incumbent (i.e., 2002 and later). When an "S" is followed by a number like a "2," "4," or "6," this represents the specific year in which this portion of the district was composed of VTDs the incumbent first represented since a redistricting occurred. For example, "S 2" means this portion of the two-party vote came from voters in VTDs that the incumbent has represented since 2002. An "R" means that this portion of the vote came from constituents who were redrawn into an incumbent's district for that specific election year.

With this classification system of VTDs according to when they were placed in an incumbent's congressional district, we can assess the duration of electoral effects due to redistricting. An example will be illuminating. Let us take the case of Chet Edwards, an Anglo Democrat who was first elected in 1990 and faced a Republican challenger in every single election from 2002 through 2010, when he was finally defeated. In 2002, among those constituents he retained prior to redistricting ("S"), Edwards won 55 percent of the two-party vote. By contrast, in 2002, among the constituents drawn into his district ("R"), Edwards took just 35 percent of the votes. In 2004, the VTDs drawn into his district in 2002 were completely removed and replaced with another set of redrawn VTDs, whose constituents gave him 46 percent of their

Table 6.3. Redistricting and Democratic Incumbent Vote Shares

Incumbent	2002		2004		2006		2008		2010	
Max Sandlin (1)	S	57	S	42						
	R	48	S 2	48						
			R	35						
Jim Turner (2)	S	63								
	R	37								
Ralph Hall (4)	S	58								
	R	69								
Nick Lampson (9, 2)	S	60	S	61						
	R	38	R	29						
Lloyd Doggett (10, 25)			S	81	S	90	S	88	S	83
			R	59	S 4	67	S 4	62	S 4	42
					R	66	S 6	61	S 6	46
Chet Edwards (11, 17)	S	55	S	63	S	65	S	60	S	46
	R	35	R	46	S 4	56	S 4	51	S 4	32
Ruben Hinojosa (15)			S	69	S	76	S	72	S	65
			R	48	S 2	69	S 2	58	S 2	43
					R	68	S 4	65	S 4	51
Silvestre Reyes (16)			S	69					S	61
			S 2	67					S 2	60
Charles Stenholm (17, 19)	S	54	S	50						
	R	40	S 2	42						
			R	36						
Sheila Jackson Lee (18)	S	77			S	80	S	78	S	71
	R	93			S 2	98	S 2	97	S 2	96
					S 4	77	S 4	81	S 4	76
Charles Gonzales (20)			S	67			S	74	S	65
			S 2	84			S 2	88	S 2	83
			R	67			S 4	73	S 4	63

Table 6.3. Continued

Incumbent	2002		2004		2006		2008		2010	
Martin Frost (24, 32)	S	70	S	74						
	R	58	S 2	79						
			R	41						
Solomon Ortiz (27)	S	62	S	66	S	61	S	62	S	52
	R	83	S 2	79	S 2	74	S 2	78	S 2	71
			R	52	S 4	48	S 4	47	S 4	37
Ciro Rodriguez (28)	S	74								
	R	62								
Henry Cuellar (28)							S	61	S	45
							S 6	82	S 6	76
Gene Green (29)					S	78	S	79	S	69
					S 4	66	S 4	66	S 4	54
E. Bernice Johnson (30)	S	77			S	89	S	90	S	86
	R	64			S 2	73	S 2	80	S 2	73
					S 4	69	S 4	68	S 4	56

Note: S = VTDs that remain in the same incumbent's district; R = VTDs drawn into a different incumbent's district. The number following "S" denotes the election year in which the VTDs first remained with the same incumbent: "S 2" = same VTDs since 2002, "S 4" = same VTDs since 2004, and "S 6" = same VTDs since 2006. The numbers shown are the incumbent's two-party percentage of the VTD vote. Data for the analysis were provided by the Texas Legislative Council.

votes. And among the constituents he represented since at least 2000 (before the 2002 redistricting), Edwards won 63 percent of the two-party vote; hence, their support kept him in office.

Edwards's District 17 (it was District 11 in 2000 and 2002) was not altered after the 2004 election. Therefore, from 2006 through 2010, his two sets of VTDs consist of those constituents he represented since 2000 (or earlier) and constituents he has represented since the 2004 redistricting, who now are denoted as "S 4," his same constituents since the 2004 election (this of course means that in 2004 they are redrawn VTDs, displayed as an "R"). In the Democratic years of 2006 and 2008, Edwards won a majority of the vote from his constituents in both the VTDs he had represented since at least 2000 and the voters in VTDs he had received since the 2004 redistricting. But in 2010, an awful year for Democrats and conversely the best year for the GOP since 1938 (in terms of national election returns), in both types of VTDs he fell short of winning majorities. Throughout this span of elections (2002–2010), we see that Edwards performed better among the constituents who resided in VTDs he represented before the 2002 redistricting. In 2010 Edwards lost a lot of support in both types of VTDs, "S" and "S 4," but his support was markedly stronger among the constituents he represented for a longer period of time (46 percent in "S" VTDs versus 32 percent in "S 4" VTDs).

Now that we have gone into detail with the example of Democratic Congressman Edwards, we can be more comprehensive in pointing out the broader effects of redistricting on Democratic incumbent vote shares from 2002 to 2010. Overall, redistricting was not kind to Democrats—especially those Anglo Democrats we have already mentioned at some length. There were ten Democratic incumbents who at some point had a category of VTDs that registered less than a majority of the vote (Sandlin, Turner, Lampson, Doggett, Edwards, Hinojosa, Stenholm, Frost, Ortiz, and Cuellar). Among Anglo Democrats, Ralph Hall and Gene Green were the only ones for whom each category of their VTDs awarded them a majority of the two-party vote.

Winning 60 percent of the two-party vote is considered a substantial victory and a sound benchmark for identifying incumbents who are electorally safe.[53] With this in mind, among the seventeen Democratic incumbents listed in Table 6.3, only four received 60 percent or more of the two-party vote in every category of VTD for each contested election they waged between 2002 and 2010: Silvestre Reyes, Sheila Jackson Lee, Charles Gonzales, and Ciro Rodriguez. In this respect, these four minority representatives were exceptional.

More common among Democratic incumbents was the presence of more recently acquired VTDs with downright hostile voters. In 2004, Nick Lampson and Martin Frost were both defeated because of their lack of support from voters in their redrawn VTDs (29 percent of the vote for Lampson and 41 percent of the vote for Frost). In 2010, Democrat Solomon Ortiz lost, which no one expected. As we see from the categorization of his votes, Ortiz was denied reelection by his most recent set of constituents, the ones who resided in the VTDs drawn into his district in 2004. The constituents residing in this portion of the district gave Ortiz just 37 percent of the two-party vote—directly contributing to his shocking defeat.

Lloyd Doggett survived the 2010 election because of the overwhelming support he drew from the constituents living in the part of the district he had represented the longest. Doggett garnered 83 percent of the vote among these residents, whereas the constituents located in the VTDs Doggett had represented since 2004 and 2006 were more supportive of his Republican challenger. Finally, a notable exception to the general pattern of Democratic incumbents performing worse among voters residing in the newer parts of their districts is Henry Cuellar. It is evident that the 2006 redistricting strengthened Cuellar's hold on District 28. In 2010 Cuellar received 45 percent of the two-party vote among the constituents he had represented since winning the open District 28 in 2004. But he won an impressive 76 percent of the vote among the residents comprising the 53 percent of his district voting age population he inherited in the 2006 redistricting.

The story of redistricting and Republican incumbent vote shares is a simpler one to tell. With one exception, the redrawing of congressional boundaries did little to place Republicans in serious electoral danger. This said, we find that Republicans, like their Democratic counterparts, also generally did best among the constituents residing in the parts of their districts they had represented the longest. Using 60 percent of the two-party vote as an indicator of a safe seat, from 2002 to 2010 six of the sixteen Republicans in Table 6.4 never received less than 60 percent of the vote in any of the classified sections of their districts (Hall, Hensarling, Barton, Brady, Granger, and Thornberry). And three incumbents actually performed as well, if not better, among the newer parts of their districts (Carter, Hensarling, and Paul).

Table 6.4. Redistricting and Republican Incumbent Vote Shares

Incumbent	2002		2004		2006		2008		2010	
Sam Johnson (3)	S	76			S	65	S	63	S	69
	R	73			S 2	64	S 2	59	S 2	67
					S 4	59	S 4	55	S 4	63
Ralph Hall (4)			S	75	S	69	S	73	S	81
			R	66	S 4	64	S 4	69	S 4	75
Jeb Hensarling (5)			S	65	S	62			S	68
			R	68	S 4	66			S 4	78
Joe Barton (6)	S	75	S	70	S	63	S	65	S	68
	R	68	S 2	66	S 2	61	S 2	62	S 2	67
			R	63	S 4	61	S 4	61	S 4	69
John Culberson (7)			S	71	S	68	S	62		
			S 2	49	S 2	57	S 2	36		
			R	62	S 4	55	S 4	54		
Kevin Brady (8)			S	82	S	77	S	80	S	86
			S 2	66	S 2	64	S 2	60	S 2	69
			R	61	S 4	60	S 4	70	S 4	78
Kay Granger (12)			S	71	S	66	S	68	S	73
			S 2	78	S 2	74	S 2	73	S 2	78
			R	67	S 4	64	S 4	63	S 4	68
Mac Thornberry (13)	S	76			S	75	S	75		
	R	86			S 2	84	S 2	84		
					S 4	66	S 4	75		
Ron Paul (14)	S	67			S	57			S	76
	R	71			S 4	62			S 4	76
Randy Neugebauer (19)			S	65	S	70	S	74	S	80
			R	52	S 4	69	S 4	75	S 4	81
Lamar Smith (21)	S	78	S	75	S	74			S	76
	R	67	S 2	64	S 2	68			S 2	66
			R	49	S 4	57			S 4	57
					R	76			S 6	74
Tom DeLay (22)	S	64	S	58						
	R	71	S 2	68						
			R	52						

Table 6.4. Continued

Incumbent	2002		2004		2006		2008		2010	
Henry Bonilla (23)	S	52	S	68	S	56				
	R	60	S 2	67	S 2	46				
			R	77	S 4	76				
					R	20				
Michael Burgess (26)			S	76	S	69	S	70	S	76
			R	55	S 4	52	S 4	51	S 4	58
John Carter (31)			S	66	S	59	S	60		
			R	67	S 4	61	S 4	64		
Pete Sessions (32)	S	49	S	50	S	46	S	57	S	58
	R	72	S 2	60	S 2	62	S 2	64	S 2	69
			R	46	S 4	50	S 4	48	S 4	54

Note: S = VTDs that remain in the same incumbent's district; R = VTDs drawn into a different incumbent's district. The number following "S" denotes the election year in which the VTDs first remained with the same incumbent: "S 2" = same VTDs since 2002, "S 4" = same VTDs since 2004, and "S 6" = same VTDs since 2006. The numbers shown are the incumbent's two-party percentage of the VTD vote. Data for the analysis were provided by the Texas Legislative Council.

Likewise, after defeating fellow incumbent Charles Stenholm in 2004, Republican Randy Neugebauer henceforth received commensurate support from the constituents he inherited in the 2004 redistricting.

Between 2002 and 2010, redistricting claimed only one Republican casualty, Representative Henry Bonilla, a member of the Texas congressional delegation since 1992, when he defeated the scandal-plagued Hispanic Democratic Congressman Albert G. Bustamante in the Texas-sized District 23 (sprawling from the western part of San Antonio to the outskirts of El Paso). The expansive majority Hispanic 23rd district was barely touched by redistricting in 2002 and then only modestly altered in 2004, in order to bolster Bonilla (see Table 6.1). Given his status as the only Republican in the Hispanic congressional delegation, Bonilla was always vulnerable to a potentially strong Hispanic Democratic challenger and his core support came not from Hispanics but rather Anglos residing in suburban San Antonio. The constituency Bonilla received in the 2004 redistricting was mostly Anglo, and these constituents gave Bonilla 77 percent of the two-party vote in 2004 and 76 percent of the vote in his unsuccessful runoff election in 2006[54] against erstwhile Democratic incumbent Ciro Rodriguez.

As shown previously in Table 6.1, only two Republicans had their districts altered in the 2006 redistricting, Bonilla and Lamar Smith in District 21. Smith was strengthened in the 2006 redistricting by the voters he inherited from Bonilla's district. The newly drawn District 21 received its constituents from Districts 23 and 28. Of these redrawn constituents, who made up 28 percent of the district voting age population, 70 percent came from District 23, and 72 percent of these redrawn residents were Anglos. By comparison, of the 30 percent of redrawn constituents who came from District 28 (represented by Democrat Henry Cuellar), 73 percent were either African American (33 percent) or Hispanic (40 percent).

The constituents Bonilla lost to Smith in 2006 were replaced by a much more Hispanic and hence Democratic contingent of voters. The redrawn constituents Bonilla received in 2006 came from Districts 21 and 28. But just 213 of these redrawn residents came from District 21; the remaining 99.9 percent (238,189 people) came from District 28, 78 percent of whom were Hispanics. Bonilla had not represented such a large portion of redrawn voters before 2006, but his general election opponent, Ciro Rodriguez, had, until he was defeated in the District 28 Democratic primary by Henry Cuellar in 2004.

In 2006, the infusion of District 28 residents into District 23 transformed its demographics. In 2004 Bonilla's district was 41 percent Anglo, 2 percent Black, 55 percent Hispanic, and 2 percent Other. In 2006, District 23 was now 30 percent Anglo, 3 percent Black, 65 percent Hispanic, and 2 percent Other. In the 2006 special runoff election against Democrat Ciro Rodriguez,

Bonilla won 46 percent of the two-party vote. It is patently clear that the 2006 redistricting ended Bonilla's congressional career. Of the 31 percent of his district voting age population redrawn in 2006, Bonilla managed to win a paltry 20 percent of the vote.

The Effects of Redistricting on Incumbent Vote Shares

In this last empirical section, we employ multivariate analysis to assess the effects of redistricting on incumbent vote shares. The unit of analysis is the Voting Tabulation District and the dependent variable is the incumbent share of the two-party vote (only contested races are included). Beyond what we show in Tables 6.3 and 6.4, this multivariate regression analysis allows us to assess the effects of redistricting on incumbent vote shares after statistically controlling for the racial composition of the Voting Tabulation District.

There are four exclusive and exhaustive categories for the racial variables: the VTD percent of the voting age population that is (1) Anglo (AVAP), (2) Black (BVAP), (3) Hispanic (HVAP), and (4) Other (OVAP). The AVAP is the omitted category or comparison group.[55] We expect that compared to the AVAP, these other racial categories will be positively related to Democratic incumbent vote shares and negatively related to Republican incumbent vote shares.

In addition to including the VTD percentage of each racial group, we weight our data based on the size of the voting age population. We also include fixed effects for the congressional district, because of the unique characteristics associated with each one. Finally, our variables of interest are a set of N-1 dummy variables that indicate when VTDs were received by each incumbent. Specifically, for each election year, the omitted variable is the set of VTDs an incumbent had represented since 2000 (or earlier), or when he was first elected to Congress since the 2000 election. These VTDs operate as the comparison group in the analysis, as in the process described above for racial groups. In other words, the base category of VTDs (the comparison group) consists of those parts of the district the incumbent has represented the longest.

The dummy variables included in each election year consist of those VTDs an incumbent received more recently as a direct consequence of redistricting. Because Texas congressional boundaries were redrawn in three consecutive elections beginning with 2002, the natural progression of dummy variables for each election from 2002 to 2010 is: (1) "Redrawn" for the 2002 election, (2) "Same 2002" and "Redrawn" for the 2004 election; (3) "Same 2002," "Same 2004," and "Redrawn" for the 2006 election, and (4) "Same 2002," "Same 2004," and "Same 2006" for both the 2008 and 2010 elections.

An example with one incumbent will make this methodology clearer. In 2002, Democratic incumbent Solomon Ortiz represented District 27. After redistricting he retained many of the same VTDs (the omitted base category in 2002) and also inherited several new VTDs (the redrawn dummy variable for 2002). In 2004, District 27 was redrawn again and now Ortiz had another set of new VTDs (the redrawn dummy variable for 2004) in addition to the VTDs he received in the 2002 redistricting (now labeled "Same 2002") and the VTDs he represented since at least 2000 (the base omitted category of VTDs). Because District 27 was not altered in 2006, the two dummy variables from 2006 through 2010 for Solomon Ortiz are labeled "Same 2002" and "Same 2004"—those VTDs that were redrawn in the 2002 redistricting (that become "Same 2002" from 2004 onward), and redrawn in the 2004 redistricting (that become "Same 2004" from 2006 onward).

By classifying VTDs according to when incumbents received them, we can determine what effect, if any, redistricting has had on their shares of the two-party vote. We expect that in most cases redistricting should negatively affect incumbent vote shares. So, based on our method of modeling the relationship between incumbent votes and redistricting, those VTDs that an incumbent inherits through redistricting should display a significant and negative coefficient when compared to the base category of VTDs—those VTDs an incumbent has represented the longest. We model these effects separately for Democratic and Republican incumbents.

We should note that since we had two instances where incumbents of opposing parties faced off in 2004, these models are run separately for each of these so-called dueling incumbents (Stenholm vs. Neugebauer in District 19 and Frost vs. Sessions in District 32). Finally, because of the emphasis we placed on the defeat of Republican Henry Bonilla, we also model his 2006 election separately. We are able to make these further distinctions in our analyses because we have a large N (8400 total VTDs).

The estimates for all of our models are displayed in Tables 6.A1 and 6.A2. Table 6.A1 presents the results for Democratic incumbents in the top half of the table and the results for Republican incumbents below. Table 6.A2 presents the estimates for the aforementioned dueling incumbents and Republican Henry Bonilla in 2006. By modeling the effects of redistricting for each election year, we can see the duration of its effects on incumbent vote shares. Further, because one or the other party was advantaged by the political climate for a specific election (2002, 2004, and 2010 were Republican years whereas 2006 and 2008 were Democratic years), we can see if this served to dampen or heighten the influence of redistricting for incumbents of a certain party for a given election year.

We begin our discussion of the regression results for incumbent Democrats. In Table 6.A1, we see that the set of VTDs redrawn into Democratic incumbent districts in 2002 persisted in reducing Democratic representatives' votes from 2002 through 2006. These VTDs do not significantly reduce Democratic incumbent votes in 2008, but they do once again in the 2010 election. More specifically, compared to the VTDs Democratic incumbents represented the longest (the base category), or since the 2000 election, VTDs drawn into their districts in 2002 reduced their share of the two-party vote by 7.8 points in 2002, 7.6 points in 2004, 9.5 points in 2006, and 4.9 points in 2010.

The single most electorally harmful redistricting occurred in 2004, when the VTDs Democratic incumbents received in this election reduced their share of the vote by 11.4 points as compared to the share of the vote they received from the VTDs they represented the longest. In 2006 these same VTDs reduced Democratic incumbent votes by 4.9 points, but thereafter (in 2008 and 2010) the VTDs Democratic representatives inherited in the 2004 redistricting no longer registered as a significantly negative effect on their share of the two-party vote. Finally, we see that those VTDs that were redrawn in 2006 had no significant effect on these Democratic incumbents' vote shares in 2006 and 2008. But in 2010, we see that compared to the VTDs these Democrats had represented the longest, the VTDs they inherited through the 2006 redistricting were actually more supportive, registering a 6-point increase in their share of the two-party vote in the 2010 election.

We can take our analysis a step further by displaying the predicted vote shares for Democratic incumbents when we set the racial variables at their mean values. In Table 6.5 we present the predicted vote shares for Democratic incumbents in each election year according to the relevant VTD category. A predicted vote share is underlined when it is significantly different from the base VTD category (designated "same" in the table), as determined from the regression results displayed in Table 6.A1.

In 2002, there is an 8-point drop in the Democratic incumbent vote share for redrawn VTDs (56 percent vs. 64 percent in same VTDs). This difference remains in 2004, and now we see that there is a 12-point reduction in the vote for VTDs drawn into the district in 2004 (52 percent vs. 64 percent in same VTDs). In 2006 the VTDs redrawn in 2002 ("same 2002") are now less supportive of Democratic incumbents at 64 percent than are the VTDs redrawn in 2004 ("same 2004") at 69 percent. And the VTDs redrawn in 2006 show the highest support for Democratic incumbents at 78 percent, but the difference is not statistically significant compared to the predicted vote share for "same" VTDs at 74 percent. In 2008, another good year for the Democratic Party, there is no statistically significant difference between "same" VTDs and any of the predicted vote shares for the other three VTD categories ("same 2002," "same 2004," and "same 2006"). In 2010, the VTDs Democratic incumbents

Table 6.5. Redistricting and Predicted Vote Shares for Democratic Incumbents

VTD	2002	VTD	2004	VTD	2006	VTD	2008	VTD	2010
same	64	same	64	same	74	same	72	same	63
redrawn	56	same 2002	56	same 2002	64	same 2002	69	same 2002	58
		redrawn 2004	52	same 2004	69	same 2004	69	same 2004	59
				redrawn 2006	78	same 2006	77	same 2006	69
N=Incumbents	11		8		7		9		10

NOTE: Predicted vote shares were computed using Clarify software (Tomz, Wittenberg, and King 2003). Estimates were derived from the corresponding regression models shown in Appendix Table 6.A1 when the racial variables (BVAP, HVAP, and OVAP) are set at their mean values. Underlined predicted vote shares designate that the value is significantly different from the predicted value for "same" VTDs.

received in 2002 are significantly less supportive vis-à-vis "same" VTDs (58 percent vs. 63 percent) and the VTDs inherited in the 2006 redistricting are six points more favorable at 69 percent to Democratic incumbents as compared to the VTDs these Democrats have represented the longest.

Turning to the predicted vote shares for Republican incumbents in Table 6.6 reveals a very different set of results than those for Democratic incumbents. The findings for the VTDs redrawn in 2002 are notable for the fact that these constituents never exhibit significantly less support for Republican incumbents than what those incumbents received from the VTDs they represented the longest. Based on these results we can say that the 2002 redistricting had no substantive effect on Republican incumbent vote shares in that specific year, or any election thereafter. By contrast, the 2004 redistricting, which was an uncompromising Republican gerrymander, involved an expansive strategy of constituency redistribution, and the constituents GOP representatives received in 2004 were markedly less supportive. Compared to the Republican incumbent vote shares in "same" VTDs, constituents redrawn in 2004 reduced Republican votes by 8 points in 2004, 6 points in 2006, and 3 points in 2008. However, by 2010, constituents residing in VTDs redrawn in 2004 ("same 2004") were not any less supportive of Republican incumbents.

We also find that in 2006, constituents redrawn into Republican districts were not significantly less supportive of Republican incumbents from a statistical standpoint, despite the difference in predicted vote shares (58 percent for "Redrawn 2006" vs. 64 percent for "same"). But as we have discussed, it is likely that this null finding is directly related to the evidence that, for the two Republicans whose districts were redrawn in 2006, one (Lamar Smith in District 21) was not harmed whereas the other (Henry Bonilla in District 23) clearly was. We cannot present the predicted Republican incumbent vote shares according to constituents redrawn in 2006 for the 2008 and 2010 elections because of our modeling specifications. First, in 2008 Henry Bonilla was no longer in Congress (he lost in 2006) and Lamar Smith ran uncontested. And second, in 2010 Lamar Smith drew a Demo-

Table 6.6. Redistricting and Predicted Vote Shares for Republican Incumbents

VTD	2002	VTD	2004	VTD	2006	VTD	2008	VTD	2010
Same	67	same	69	same	64	same	65	same	70
Redrawn	66	same 2002	66	same 2002	62	same 2002	64	same 2002	68
		redrawn 2004	61	same 2004	58	same 2004	62	same 2004	69
				redrawn 2006	58				
N=Incumbents	8		11		15		11		11

Note: Predicted vote shares were computed using Clarify software (Tomz, Wittenberg, and King 2003). Estimates were derived from the corresponding regression models shown in Appendix Table 6.A1 when the racial variables (BVAP, HVAP, and OVAP) are set at their mean values. Underlined predicted vote shares designate that the value is significantly different from the predicted value for "same" VTDs.

cratic challenger, but since we include fixed effects for each congressional district, the "Same 2006" dummy is perfectly collinear with the district fixed effect because all of the relevant "same 2006" VTDs reside in District 21.

Our last batch of findings concerns the two sets of dueling incumbents in 2004 and Republican Henry Bonilla's district in 2006. First, we consider the effects of redistricting separately for each incumbent who was pitted against another in the 2004 elections: (1) Democrat Charles Stenholm in District 19, (2) Republican Randy Neugebauer in District 19, (3) Democrat Martin Frost in District 32, and (4) Republican Pete Sessions in District 32. The regression results for these incumbents (along with the results in 2006 for Republican Bonilla) are displayed in Table 6.A2.

In 2004, the redrawn District 19 was composed of VTDs that were from Districts 19, 17, and 13 in the 2002 elections. In 2002, Democrat Charles Stenholm represented District 17, Republican Mac Thornberry represented District 13, and, after winning the 2003 special election to fill the seat vacated by veteran Republican Larry Combest, Randy Neugebauer became the incumbent in District 19. In the first model shown in Table 6.A2 for Democrat Charles Stenholm, he did much worse among all three sets of his more recently acquired VTDs: the VTDs he received in the 2002 redistricting, the VTDs drawn into his district in 2004 that came from District 13 (represented by Mac Thornberry), and the VTDs represented by Randy Neugebauer.

Republican Congressman Neugebauer, because he was first elected in 2002, only had two sets of more recent VTDs, both acquired in the 2004 redistricting: the VTDs that came from Thornberry's District 13 and the VTDs that came from Stenholm's District 17. Like Stenholm, Neugebauer received significantly less support from constituents residing in the VTDs he received in the 2004 redistricting (and does much worse among Stenholm's constituents).

The third and fourth columns of regression estimates in Table 6.A2 show the effects of redistricting on the vote shares of incumbents Frost and Sessions, who faced each other in District 32 in 2004. For Democratic Congressman Frost we see that he performed significantly worse among the VTDs he received in the 2002 redistricting and the VTDs he inherited in 2004, which are separated in terms of those represented by Republican Pete Sessions in 2002 and all of the other VTDs that were not in Frost's district before the 2004 election.[56]

For Republican Congressman Pete Sessions, we have changed the set of VTD dummies because the district he has represented since the 2002 election, District 32, is a better indicator of his core supporters. In other words, the base category of VTDs for Sessions is that of the VTDs he received in the 2002 redistricting. We set up the model this way for Sessions because he left District 5 in 2002 and sought reelection in the new District 32, which included just 15 percent of the voting age population that had resided in District 5 in 2000. Unlike Frost, Sessions performs more poorly among his longest-represented VTDs ("same 2000") and he actually performs better among constituents whom he inherited in 2004 that were not represented by Frost in 2002 ["Redrawn (Other)"]. And not surprisingly, Sessions experiences a significant reduction in his vote share among the VTDs Frost represented in 2002 ["Redrawn (Frost)"].

Finally, the last column in Table 6.A2 shows the regression estimates for Republican Congressman Henry Bonilla in 2006. The effects of redistricting might appear contrary to what we would expect given the findings presented in Table 6.4. Recall that in 2006, as shown in Table 6.4, Bonilla received 56 percent of the vote among his "same" VTDs, 46 percent in "same 2002" VTDs, 76 percent in "same 2004" VTDs, and only 20 percent in "redrawn" VTDs. In the multivariate estimates in Table 6.A2, we find that compared to his "same" VTDs, Bonilla did significantly better among the VTDs he received in the 2002 redistricting, and there is no difference in the support he received from the VTDs he inherited in the 2004 redistricting. These estimates appear questionable based on what we know from the results in Table 6.4. There is, however, an explanation for these unexpected findings. We are assessing the effects of redistricting with the VTD as the unit of analysis, and in the case of District 23 in 2006, there are not enough VTDs categorized as "same 2002" (n = 3) and "same 2004" (n = 1) to deem their influence (or lack thereof) reliable and valid. By contrast, there are plenty of VTDs classified as "redrawn" in 2006 (n = 77) and therefore the negative effect these VTDs have on Bonilla's vote share is reliable and valid.

Table 6.7 presents the predicted vote shares for our dueling incumbents and Congressman Bonilla in 2006 when we set the racial variables in these models at their mean values. Congressman Stenholm was crushed by the presence of VTDs drawn into his district in 2002 (36 percent) and 2004 (40 percent among erstwhile Thornberry VTDs and 36 percent among Neugebauer VTDs), and Congressman Neugebauer did not obtain a majority among the VTDs Stenholm represented (46 percent), but only dropped off a little in the case of VTDs that Congressman Thornberry previously represented (60 percent of the vote).

Frost was denied reelection by the two sets of VTDs he received in 2004 (49 percent in Sessions VTDs and 46 percent in Other VTDs), and conversely Sessions was victorious thanks to the support he garnered from the VTDs he represented since the 2002 redistricting (51 percent) and the Other VTDs he inherited in the 2004 redistricting (54 percent of the vote). Finally, we see that after controlling for VTD racial composition, Republican Henry Bonilla received a meager 33 percent of the votes of constituents drawn into his district in 2006, hence these were the voters who ended his fourteen-year congressional career.

Conclusion

Ever since the *Baker v. Carr* (1962) decision mandating equal population, Texas has been an important player in the legal and electoral controversies that surround redistricting practices.[57] In this chapter, we set about to demonstrate the significant electoral effects of multiple redistrictings over the course of the last decade in Texas. As we have shown, by disrupting (or not disrupting) the electoral relationship between incumbents and their

Table 6.7. Predicted Vote Shares for Dueling Incumbents in 2004, and Bonilla in 2006

Stenholm (D)	2004	Neugebauer (R)	2004	Frost (D)	2004	Sessions (R)	2004	Bonilla (R)	2010
same	54	same	64	same	63	same 2002	51	same	47
same 2002	36	Thornberry	60	same 2002	56	same	37	same 2002	60
Thornberry	40	Stenholm	46	Sessions	49	Frost	38	same 2004	36
Neugebauer	36			other VTDs	46	other VTDs	54	redrawn	33

Note: Predicted vote shares were computed using Clarify software (Tomz, Wittenberg, and King 2003). Estimates were derived from the corresponding regression models shown in Appendix Table 6.A2 when the racial variables (BVAP, HVAP, and OVAP) are set at their mean values. Underlined predicted vote shares designate that the value is significantly different from the predicted value for "same" VTDs (or "same 2002" in the case of Sessions in 2004).

longtime constituents, redistricting decision-makers can significantly alter election outcomes.

When the Democrat-controlled state House of Representatives and Republican-controlled state Senate failed to proffer a new congressional plan for the 2002 elections in Texas, a three-judge federal court, compelled by equal population requirements set forth by the U.S. Supreme Court in *Baker v. Carr* (1962) and *Wesberry v. Sanders* (1964), enacted their own plan. Causing relatively little disruption of the incumbent-constituent relationship by placing the new districts where the growth in population occurred, their ruling had the effect of prolonging the Democratic incumbency advantage secured by a Democratic gerrymander enacted ten years earlier. Of course, U.S. Supreme Court precedents warranted federal court involvement because the state legislature had failed to act. Nevertheless, the three-judge trial court's action (or relative inaction) in 2002 allowed a number of Anglo Democrats to hang on for another election cycle.

While the federal court made minimal changes to electoral lines in 2002, the Republican legislature drastically altered lines and thus the representational relationship between many constituents and their congressmen for the 2004 elections. Democratic state legislators were well aware of this negative potential, which is why they fled the state on two separate occasions in order to deny Republicans a quorum. Indeed, voters redrawn into new districts in the 2004 Republican gerrymander turned out to be less supportive of their new incumbent congressmen. Although this was true for both Democratic and Republican incumbents, the reduced support for Democratic incumbents among redrawn voters in 2004 was enough to end their congressional careers.

The courts played a central role in the process in Texas in the 2000s. As noted previously, the lower federal trial court controlled by Republican-appointed judges upheld the validity of the GOP gerrymander over the dissent of the Democratic-appointed judge. The U.S. Supreme Court, after two reviews of the case, eventually decided that the VRA had been violated and ordered the redrawing of lines yet again, leaving the task largely up to the discretion of the three-judge lower court. It is unclear why Justice Anthony Kennedy sided with the liberal minority in order to cast aside some of the Republican state legislature's handiwork from 2004. But one cannot help but believe that Kennedy was troubled by the extreme partisan gerrymander (perhaps precipitating the initial remand order in light of *Vieth*) along with the newfound concept of swapping out a majority-minority district in one part of the state (District 23) for another, less compact and more artificial majority-minority district in a different part of the state (District 25, a bacon-strip configuration that typically would not even be required by the VRA given the district's lack of compactness in the 2004 re-redistricting). As we have illustrated in this chapter, the bevy of redrawn voters placed into Congressman Bonilla's district in 2006 were responsible for his electoral defeat. The actions of the redistricting decision-makers in 2006—this time, the federal courts—contributed directly to this election outcome.

And though some political scientists are skeptical of the supposed long-term effects of redistricting,[58] by focusing on Texas and its multiple redistrictings, we are able to illustrate how the behavior of redrawn voters produces electoral effects that linger throughout a decade, well past the initial redistricting election cycle. And such large effects naturally should draw policymakers toward the difficult questions of how or whether we should undergo redistricting in furtherance of a better democracy. Some legal scholars, such as Sanford Levinson,[59] have suggested that we should move toward a proportional system of representation so as to avoid the limitless fights over redistricting and the impracticality of the one person, one vote standard (in which line-drawers might be using old population data well into a decade to achieve little more than theoretically equal populations, since district populations are not static).

Other good-government types have looked to redistricting commissions as the panacea for neutralizing the electoral effects of redistricting.[60] However, redistricting commissions, depending on their construction, are not without fault either.[61] Certainly, this chapter also provides stark evidence for the influence of the federal courts in redistricting. One could view the federal courts' role in the 2006 Texas redistricting as having a moderating impact on the partisan-controlled Republican process of 2004, but one cannot ignore the partisan favoritism exhibited by the federal judges in the lower courts, even if such partisan favoritism was inadvertent.

The Democrat-dominated 2001 federal panel kept the 1991 Democratic gerrymander largely intact (though it should be noted that the Republican appointee went along with the decision). The Republican-controlled Texas Supreme Court also intervened in the process in order to keep a Democratic state trial judge from implementing a plan that Republicans feared would be even more partisan than what would come out of a federal court. Meanwhile, the Republican-appointee-dominated federal panel in 2004 affirmed the Republican gerrymander over the vigorous dissent of the lone Democratic appointee, thus biding time for the Republican plan to go into effect for the 2004 elections before it was later overturned by the U.S. Supreme Court in 2006.

In essence, the federal courts had almost as much of a role in the electoral effects of Texas redistricting in the 2000s as did the state legislature. Whether the state and federal courts' roles were positive or negative is a normative question beyond the scope of this chapter, but the consequences of their actions (or inactions) alongside the state legislature's are evident in the electoral effects displayed here. In the wake of the 2010 census, the lower federal courts and the U.S. Supreme Court have been invited back into Texas's redistricting battles, and the courts may once again play a decisive role in how the line-drawing affects election outcomes.[62]

Texas has a long and rich history of providing plenty of evidence that allows scholars to better understand the nature and effects of redistricting and the forces that drive it. In this chapter we have relied on a unique data set that enables us to assess the electoral effects of multiple redistrictings over the span of five consecutive elections. Specifically, with these data we were able to isolate the role of redistricting in affecting the vote shares of Democratic and Republican incumbents for the duration of their time in office from 2002 through 2010. Our findings make it abundantly clear that redistricting has a considerable impact on election outcomes and not just for one single election—its influence often endures for two and sometimes even three election cycles. Time will tell if the next chapter of Texas congressional redistricting is as dynamic and consequential as the last decade has been.

In the continuing debate over how we should craft electoral lines and thus influence our democratic processes, Texas congressional redistricting in the 2000s is an important case study. The interplay of courts and legislatures in the Lone Star State over the drawing of district lines and their attendant electoral consequences has spawned considerable controversy over this hyper-political activity. The contentiousness of Texas redistricting persists, as evident in the legal back-and-forth over the 2012 congressional map while the clock ticked toward the state primaries. We will leave the particulars of this latest battle for Gary Keith in the conclusion.

Table 6.A1. Regression Results for Democratic and Republican Incumbents, 2002–2010

Democrats	2002	2004	2006	2008	2010
constant	.468*** (.026)	.372*** (.059)	.511*** (.061)	.397 (.054)	.210** (.063)
BVAP	.533*** (.035)	.603*** (.071)	.497*** (.069)	.637 (.058)	.817*** (.065)
HVAP	.320*** (.048)	.437*** (.067)	.304*** (.058)	.429 (.056)	.557*** (.070)
OVAP	−.618*** (.150)	−.292 (.294)	.109 (.269)	.220 (.231)	.317 (.334)
same 2002		−.076** (.024)	−.095** (.022)	−.025 (.018)	−.049** (.018)
same 2004			−.049* (.029)	−.026 (.027)	−.046 (.033)
same 2006				.049 (.022)	.060** (.026)
redrawn	−.078*** (.019)	−.114** (.031)	.040 (.039)		
R^2	.59	.67	.55	.68	.68
N	3,111	1,996	1,641	2,146	2,313

Republicans	2002		2004		2006		2008		2010
constant	.918***	constant	.852***	constant	.819***	constant	.874***	constant	.929***
	(.029)		(.014)		(.021)		(.013)		(.012)
BVAP	-.683***	BVAP	-.676***	BVAP	-.610***	BVAP	-.881***	BVAP	-.927***
	(.072)		(.099)		(.073)		(.061)		(.074)
HVAP	-.607***	HVAP	-.318***	HVAP	-.452***	HVAP	-.460***	HVAP	-.474***
	(.085)		(.035)		(.060)		(.049)		(.057)
OVAP	-.328**	OVAP	-.393**	OVAP	-.278**	OVAP	-.656***	OVAP	-.614***
	(.092)		(.099)		(.110)		(.103)		(.135)
redrawn	-.009	same 2002	-.031	same 2002	-.015	same 2002	-.011	same 2002	-.020
	(.031)		(.025)		(.018)		(.020)		(.021)
		redrawn	-.079**	same 2004	-.057**	same 2004	-.036**	same 2004	-.013
			(.025)		(.020)		(.019)		(.017)
				redrawn	-.059				
					(.091)				
R^2	.64		.53		.54		.73		.71
N	2,266		2,957		4,159		3,035		3,020

Note: Cell entries are OLS regression coefficients with robust standard errors in parentheses (clustered on the congressional district). Data are weighted by the VTD voting age population. The dependent variable is the incumbent's VTD percentage of the two-party vote. Only two-party contested districts are included in the models. BVAP = Black voting age population; HVAP = Hispanic voting age population; OVAP = Other voting age population. The Anglo percent of the VTD voting age population is the omitted category.

***p ≤ .001; **p ≤ .05; *p ≤ .10 (one-tailed). Given the expectation that incumbents will receive a lower percentage of the vote among constituents in redrawn VTDs, the probability that this difference is not statistically significant is denoted above by the number of asterisks; less than 10% (p<.10), less than 5% (p<.05), and less than 1% (p<.01).

Table 6.A2. Regression Results for Dueling Incumbents in 2004, and Bonilla in 2006

Stenholm (D)	2004 Neugebauer (R)	2004 Frost (D)	2004 Sessions (R)	2004 Bonilla (R)	2006
constant	.414*** constant (.010)	.768*** constant (.012)	.446*** constant (.024)	.705*** constant (.012)	.985*** constant (.029)
BVAP	.709*** BVAP (.051)	−.711*** BVAP (.052)	.804*** BVAP (.072)	−.788*** BVAP (.065)	−.398** BVAP (.137)
HVAP	.290*** HVAP (.025)	−.273*** HVAP (.025)	.306*** HVAP (.026)	−.323*** HVAP (.025)	−.736*** HVAP (.036)
OVAP	.138 OVAP (.197)	−.173 OVAP (.202)	.010 OVAP (.088)	−.060 OVAP (.083)	−1.218*** OVAP (.271)
same 2002	−.180*** redrawn (Thornberry) (.045)	−.043** same 2002 (.015)	−.070* same 2000 (.046)	−.138*** same 2002 (.030)	.132** same 2002 (.065)
redrawn (Thornberry)	−.148*** redrawn (Stenholm) (.017)	−.179*** redrawn (Sessions) (.010)	−.137*** redrawn (Frost) (.020)	−.133*** same 2004 (.018)	−.116 same 2004 (.250)
redrawn (Neugebauer)	−.187*** (.010)	redrawn (Other)	−.175*** redrawn (Other) (.019)	.034** redrawn (.012)	−.142*** redrawn (.017)
adjusted R²	.63	.61	.81	.83	.74
N	376	376	181	181	315

Note: Cell entries are OLS regression coefficients with standard errors in parentheses. Data are weighted by the VTD voting age population. The dependent variable is the incumbent's VTD percentage of the two-party vote. Only two-party contested districts are included in the models. BVAP = Black voting age population; HVAP = Hispanic voting age population; OVAP = Other voting age population. The Anglo percent of the VTD voting age population is the omitted category.

***p ≤ .001; **p ≤ .05; *p ≤ .10 (one-tailed). Given the expectation that incumbents will receive a lower percentage of the vote among constituents in redrawn VTDs, the probability that this difference is not statistically significant is denoted above by the number of asterisks; less than 10% (p<.10), less than 5% (p<.05), and less than 1% (p<.01)

Conclusion. Redistricting Redux:
2011 and Beyond

GARY A. KEITH

We began this book by noting that redistricting brawls are the quintessential American game of politics. The reader might hope that the Texas redistricting experiences covered in this book could be seen as a 40-year wilderness experience from which we have emerged and survived. We, however, do not mean to deceive: redistricting is more like the 1993 movie *Groundhog Day*, a never ending and frustrating escapade. While any decade's redistricting *could* chart new paths, the six chapters in this book demonstrate the ruts that have been cut and have deepened since 1962 and that will likely continue to guide the outcomes in this decade and beyond. The 2010 census triggered the current round of redistrictings, and as we write in 2012, the end zone for the Texas congressional and legislative redistrictings is not in sight. We cannot do a full and robust analysis of this cycle—indeed, if history is to be trusted, the 2011 redistricting may not be completed for some years to come.

2012—*Not* the End of the World (of Redistricting)

The 2010 census counted 25,145,561 Texans, up a phenomenal 20.6 percent from the 2000 count of 20,851,820.[1] As a result, Texas was the big winner in the 2010 reapportionment, gaining four additional U.S. House seats; the size of the state legislature did not change, so the equalized district population size simply grew for the state legislative seats. The mandate to increase Texas's congressional representation from 32 districts to 36 presented a much easier political task than that faced by the ten states that lost seats (Illinois, Iowa, Louisiana, Massachusetts, Michigan, Missouri, New Jersey, New York, Ohio, and Pennsylvania). Congressional seats are now huge districts—the equalized size is 698,488.

The partisan and VRA dynamics assure that the bruising battles from the 2001 and 2003 redistrictings are reinvigorated in this decade's sparring, as power blocs defend their turf and seek to maximize their seats. The political and demographic realities facing the legislature in 2011 were that Republicans were in control of redistricting (with majorities in both chambers as well as having control of the governorship and the LRB) and that the massive increase in minority voters (especially Hispanics) ensured that this group was the focus in the reconfiguring of districts.

By now, the redistricting playbook is well scripted, dog-eared, and worn. The first federal lawsuit, filed during the legislative session, was a north Texas challenge to the 2010 census figures (though this time the argument was one to exclude undocumented aliens from the count).[2] The Mexican American Legislative Caucus (MALC) then filed a state court suit in Hidalgo County, arguing that the census had undercounted Latinos).[3] Houston State Representative Harold Dutton, along with Shannon Perez and others, filed a federal suit in San Antonio, alleging constitutional issues with the census count, with Perez as the lead plaintiff (and this volume's David Richards as attorney).[4] MALC then followed with a federal suit in San Antonio (with this volume's José Garza as attorney), alleging VRA violations in the use of the census data for redistricting purposes.[5] Republican Congressman Joe Barton filed a state lawsuit in north Texas on the issue of congressional districts, attempting to establish a venue for the decade's litigation in his backyard.[6] And all of this was before any bills had passed in the legislature!

By May 30, the end of the regular session of the 82nd Legislature, the legislature approved HB 150, redistricting the state House, and SB 31, redistricting the state Senate. (And Governor Perry signed them into law.) The legislature did not finish congressional redistricting, so Perry called a special session that began May 31; legislators quickly passed SB 4, approving congressional districts.

So, what did the three plans do? By now, legislatures know that they must adhere to the equal-sized districts standard (particularly for Congress). With computers, that is now easy. Issues of compactness, communities of interest, partisanship, and minority representation/retrogression continue to provide the spice. As expected, the majority bloc in the legislature passed plans to extend and maximize its representation. This time around, it was Republican majorities that dominated and assured district lines that would protect their incumbents and increase their numbers. The huge hurdle, though, was that most of the state's population growth was due to increases in the Hispanic population—a population that is determinedly Democratic. Thus, the question was whether the Republican majority could craft districts that protected and expanded Republican numbers without repeating the disaster/boomerang that hit them with the Bonilla district in the 2003 redistricting.

The San Antonio venue would end up being the three-judge court for this decade's litigation. U.S. District Judge Orlando Garcia (a Democrat and former state representative, appointed by Clinton) was assigned the case, then Fifth Circuit Chief Judge Edith Jones filled out the three-judge court with U.S. District Judge Xavier Rodriguez (a Republican and former member of the Texas Supreme Court, appointed to the federal bench by George W. Bush), and 5th Circuit Judge Jerry Smith (a Republican appointed by Reagan). Thus, while the panel was majority Republican, it was also comprised of a Hispanic majority—a first.

The original lawsuits were then joined by a cascade of lawsuits and litigants: the Texas Latino Redistricting Task Force, the City of Austin, the NAACP, LULAC, Travis County, State Representative Marc Veasey, State Senator Wendy Davis, and others. The San Antonio court soon consolidated some of the federal suits, with *Perez* as the lead case. Thus, a plethora of plaintiff attorneys had horses in the race, including David Richards, Nina Perales, José Garza, Gerry Hebert, Chad Dunn, Renea Hicks, Rolando Rios, and Michael Hull. The lead attorney for Texas Attorney General Greg Abbott was David Schenck, an appellate lawyer who had previously clerked for the Chief Judge of the Fifth Circuit.

Meanwhile, the state had to proceed on the Voting Rights Act Section 5 preclearance requirement. Attorney General Abbott decided that the D.C. District Court provided a potentially more favorable venue than President Obama's Department of Justice (DOJ), so in July 2011 Texas filed suit, asking for a three-judge VRA panel. District Judge Rosemary Collyer (a George W. Bush appointee) got the case, then Chief Judge David Sentelle of the D.C. Circuit Court named to the three-judge panel Circuit Judge Thomas Griffith (a George W. Bush appointee), and District Judge Beryl Howell (an Obama appointee).

Soon, the DOJ weighed in, alleging that the state Senate redistricting lines passed muster under the VRA, but that the House and congressional lines did not. The DOJ ruled that both the House and congressional maps had discriminatory effects, with retrogression of minority representation and, ominously for the state, discriminatory intent. Would the D.C. court find similarly or not?

Attorney General Abbott, having to battle on two fronts, decided to try a quick audible. He asked the D.C. panel to issue a summary judgment preclearing the three plans, which, if issued, could serve to steer the San Antonio court. But his plan backfired. The D.C. court issued an order denying the summary judgment and went further, writing that:

> the Court finds and concludes that the State of Texas used an improper standard or methodology to determine which districts afford minority voters the ability to elect their preferred candidates of choice and that there are material issues of fact in dispute that prevent this Court from entering declaratory judgment that the three redistricting plans meet the requirements of Section 5 of the Voting Rights Act.[7]

With this directive, the San Antonio court continued with its trial and began considering "interim" maps for the 2012 election. The court and the litigants faced pressure as the March 6 primary and its December filing deadline approached. From the perspective of the federal court in San Antonio, if the legislature's plan had not yet been precleared by the DC court, the court was obliged to act, if Texas was to have a plan in place in time for the 2012 elections. Thus, Judges Rodriguez and Garcia (with Judge Smith partially dissenting) created interim plans for use in the 2012 elections, redrawing a map more favorable for Democrats and Hispanic plaintiff groups, and pushing the primaries to April 3. Judge Smith argued that his two colleagues should have given more deference to the state legislature's original plan in the crafting of the interim districts.

Abbott appealed to the U.S. Supreme Court for an immediate stay of the interim district order. He argued that, absent a final decision on the preclearance issue, the legislature's plans must be followed; plaintiffs filed back, telling the Supreme Court that in the absence of precleared plans, interim plans must be used—that otherwise, the Court would be creating incentives for states to simply stall preclearance and run elections with flawed plans.

The U.S. Supreme Court ruled in Abbott's favor, overturning the court plan, suggesting that the lower court judges did not give due deference to the state legislature in crafting the districts. Yet, the Supreme Court offered the lower federal court in Texas little guidance on how to draw a new plan. And thus, the saga continues in Texas redistricting between the courts and the Texas legislature. The San Antonio court reopened the case and pressed the parties to negotiate over the plans, in order to save the April 3 primary. The parties still could not come to agreement, and the court pushed the primary back to the end of May. At that point, some agreements were reached and presented to the court. On February 28, the court handed down its revised plans for Congress and the Texas House, improving Hispanic representation over the legislature's plans, but preserving Republican dominance overall. Whatever plan eventually does become law, it is sure to have significant effects on Republican and Democratic incumbents for the rest of this decade—and is being closely watched as the benchmark redistricting case law for states across the nation as they, too, get in line for preclearance and for court action.

Meanwhile, the D.C. court began its full trial on the question of Section 5 preclearance of Texas's plans. Yet the court slow-marched its hearing, then put the decision on the back burner—assuring that the San Antonio court's revised districts would have to be used for the 2012 elections, while the D.C. court continued to mull over the VRA issues for the longer term. Finally after the primaries, in late August 2012—more than a year after its initial ruling—the court denied preclearance to the plans.[8] The court found that the state had failed to show its maps to be nondiscriminatory. The judges had sharp criticism for Texas, ruling that in specified districts the legislature had failed the retrogression test of the VRA: under the maps, Hispanic voters had a realistic chance to elect candidates of their choice in fewer districts than under the existing system. Attorney General Abbott vowed to appeal immediately to the Supreme Court—and indeed in both the redistricting case and a parallel photo/voter-identification case, he suggested a frontal assault against the constitutionality of the Voting Rights Act. Thus, again, a Texas case may serve as the vehicle for the U.S. Supreme Court to affirm or alter the redistricting landscape.

Epilogue: Navigating the Brambles of the Political Thicket

GARY A. KEITH

We have argued that a multidisciplinary approach would help us better understand Texas redistricting. Thus, the seven authors herein have used historical, legal, institutional/legislative, political/sociological, and analytical/empirical approaches to describe, analyze, and explain Texas redistricting.

Social scientists value theory building. Collectively herein, ours is more a Cautionary Tale than a Grand Theory—and perhaps we will never have enough knowledge to build a theory of redistricting, but our approaches in looking at forty years of redistricting in Texas can at least produce a boilerplate for such analysis. The descriptions and analyses in this book's six chapters serve to produce the following ten Redistricting Rules to use in watching as this decade's redistricting develops. Most of these rules should also be useful in examining and comparing redistricting efforts in other states—and for future redistrictings as well.

1. The Legislative Cooks Choose and Mix the Ingredients

If the legislature is the kitchen of redistricting, then the legislative players are the cooks who control the ingredients thrown into the stew. Winburn noted the goal of incumbent protection and partisan advance,[1] but there are also players (state legislators as well as congressmen, who are often former Texas legislators) seeking to advance their own careers or destroy the careers of opponents. The 1965 redistricting rewarded Republican effort by "locking" a district for George H. W. Bush. State Representative Bob Eckhardt played the game skillfully enough to carve out a congressional district for himself. The 1971 legislature reacted against the invasion of Republicans and crafted districts to defeat the Republican congressmen. The 1981 legislature, because of internal politics, gubernatorial intervention, and partisan animosity, went after Democratic Congressman Jim Mattox and stripped away his district. The 2003 legislature—the first with a Republican Senate and House—carved out a district to assure defeat of the chair of the U.S. House Democratic Congressional Campaign Committee, Martin Frost. The 2011 legislature tried to finish one of the jobs that they attempted unsuccessfully in 2003—crafting districts to oust Austin's Democratic Congressman Lloyd Doggett. In 2003, they had carved Austin into three districts, but Doggett still won from one of them; in 2011, they split Austin five ways, making it virtually impossible for Doggett to have constituents who knew him, which McKee and McKenzie demonstrated is crucial in redistricting and reelection. (Yet Doggett defied the odds and won the primary anyway.)

2. Redistricting Action Must Be Incentivized

The legislature did not redistrict itself or Congress early in the twentieth century because there was a big disincentive to redistricting—it would result in losses for the dominant power. While the rules of the game have changed, the incentive/disincentive dynamic is ever present. In the 1980s, the courts forced changes that the Democratic legislature did not like—so after the 1982 election with the court plans, the 1983 legislature had incentive to come back and adopt plans to replace the court plans with their own. In 2001, the presence of a Democratic House alongside a Republican Senate, a Republican governor, and a Republican LRB created an incentive for the legislature to *not* redistrict:

passing House and congressional bills would require compromise between Democrats and Republicans to get bills through the House; stalling and not redistricting would allow the all-Republican forum of the LRB (and likely Republican courts) to make the redistricting decisions. Thus, sometimes there is an incentive for the legislature to act to keep other actors out; other times, there is an incentive to stall legislative action and steer redistricting into the more favorable forum of the LRB and/or the courts.

3. "Communities" are in the Eye of the Legislative Beholder

"Compactness" of districts is a judicial principle aimed at putting some boundaries around gerrymandering. Communities of interest should be kept together when possible. Yet in state after state, political considerations, VRA considerations, and case outcomes have led to elongated, twisting districts that rival the original gerrymander. Compactness no longer appears to be a primary goal—indeed, the Texas constitutional requirement of keeping counties intact can now be suspended when other factors trump it. Rather than providing representation by close-knit geographic communities, legislative cooks often have different kinds of communities in mind—partisan communities or racial/ethnic communities.

4. Legislators Go About as Far as They Can Go

As both David Richards and J. D. Pauerstein suggested, redistricting is a game of the dominant power bloc maximizing its power base. So, if legislators have the votes, they pass plans that provide the maximum representation for their bloc, guesstimating the legal and political viability of line placement, then crossing their fingers, hiring lawyers, and hoping that the courts let them go that far. The 1965 court concurring opinion in *Bush v. Martin* said that the plan was "the most discriminatory plan presented," but that the legislative remedy is best rather than a court plan.[2] In 2012, the Supreme Court ruled similarly.

5. Legislators Design Districts for the Decade—and Beyond!

Electoral effects of a redistricting are likely to endure beyond one election—districting does not have just a one-election shelf life. In Chapter 4, J. D. Pauerstein suggests that "players seek to design the field for future rounds of the electoral game." Savvy redistricting includes long-term strategizing: designing for the decade and beyond. Computer tailoring of districts serves to heighten the level of confidence in future outcomes. Moreover, as McKee and McKenzie argue, district lines can be crafted and recrafted in ways that affect the constituent-legislator bond, which in turn influences electoral odds over numerous elections. Redistricting alters the relationship between voters and representatives, potentially nullifying the incumbency advantage that carries legislators to victory, cycle after cycle.

6. Timeclock Management is Crucial to the Game

Census figures become available to the legislature in the midst of its 140-day session of an odd-numbered year. Bills must be crafted and politicked through in a relatively short period of time. Then, all the players know that the election period needs to begin by about December of that year, when filing deadlines roll around. Yet litigation often wreaks havoc with that timeline. Thus, legislators and litigators craft their strategy of finding a favorable judicial forum and jumping into it as early as possible, applying for or delaying VRA preclearance actions depending on the political shape of the landscape, and possibly forcing the courts to impose interim plans just for the imminent election. The ticking clock sometimes goes off before action is completed, though. Courts had to roll back filing deadlines in nearly every decade since the political thicket was opened to court action, including in the current round.

7. Forum Shopping Shapes the Battle

In Chapter 3, David Richards commented that the mother's milk of redistricting lawsuits is forum shopping. Both his chapter and Pauerstein's describe the practice of litigators filing "placeholder suits" in counties that might provide a favorable judge in order to be ready before the ink is even dry on the new redistricting law. Thus, in each decade (including the current one), there are numerous early suits from Democratic and Republican litigators, each vying to be the ultimate vehicle for resolution of the battle. McKee and McKenzie describe the importance of predicting judges' partisan and ideological influences in the final outcomes of redistricting battles—and particularly in interpretations of VRA preclearance standards.

8. The State Plays Preclearance Chess with the Feds

Section 5 of the Voting Rights Act creates two potential avenues for winning preclearance of redistricting plans: through the Department of Justice or through the U.S. District Court of D.C. The DOJ—rightly or wrongly—is perceived as a tool of the president and attorney general in defending their party. Thus, if Texas is governed by the same party as the president, there is an incentive to go the DOJ avenue for preclearance; if not, the D.C. court is seen as offering higher odds. For instance, in 1981, Republican Governor Bill Clements and his secretary of state went to President Reagan's DOJ, which sided with them against the Democratic legislature's plan, denying preclearance. In 1993, the (Democratic) legislature came into special session to undo the court redistricting plans—then went to the D.C. court for preclearance rather than to President Bush's DOJ. And in

2011, Republican Attorney General Greg Abbott filed with the court rather than asking President Obama's DOJ for preclearance. As he learned, there is no guarantee of the outcome, but the actors must play the odds.

9. Both Sides Play Chicken with the Courts

Three-judge court decisions on redistricting are appealable directly to the U.S. Supreme Court. And Texas litigators have become frequent flyers in getting the Court to accept their redistricting cases! First, the legislature plays chicken by aggressively redistricting to the dominant bloc's maximum advantage; then litigator-negotiators go through forum shopping and, if successful, get a three-judge court to approve a plan with sharp edges; thus they are engaging in a game of guesstimating the higher court's position on giving its stamp of approval to court plan aggressiveness vs. legislative plan aggressiveness. In *White v. Weiser*[3] the Supreme Court wrote that the trial court should not preempt the legislative task nor intrude more than necessary. Often these battles involve VRA dynamics. In *Seamon v. Upham*,[4] Judge William Wayne Justice wrote that Governor Clements's victory in creating a Black Dallas congressional district was an illegal racial gerrymander; in *Bush v. Vera*,[5] the Supreme Court ruled that three Democratic districts were illegal racial gerrymanders. In 2011, Hispanic and Democratic litigators first won a favorable plan from the three-judge court, but then lost when the Supreme Court sided with the legislature rather than the court.

10. The Dominant Player Creates or Divides Coalitions to Push to Final Victory

Winning final authoritative declaration of redistricting plans often requires negotiations, coalition politicking, and compromise. Parties, governors, legislators, and/or litigators work to create coalitions of convenience or to divide existing coalitions in order to win final political support. This hardball politicking can involve racial/ethnic or geographic communities, and may disrupt partisan communities. In 1965, Democratic State Representative Bob Eckhardt worked with George Bush and Republican lawyers to craft the "Eckhardt/Republican" Plan that ultimately won the day. Craig Washington argued that redistricting is often a tool of disenfranchisement of "out" groups. He described the Houston battles involving the parties and African Americans, Mexican Americans, and Anglos and told his fellow Democrats that the Republican plan to put white Democrats against minority Democrats was "political mischief." Pauerstein, Washington, and Richards each discussed the 1981 experience of Governor Clements pushing for the creation of a Black congressional district in Dallas—from the opposing goals of enhancing minority representation versus splitting the Democratic coalition.

In 2012, when the three-judge panel was compelled to redraw its plan, Republican Attorney General Abbott and the Texas Latino Redistricting Task Force negotiated to produce plans that could be to the advantage of each. When the court issued its revised plan, Nina Perales, MALDEF vice president of litigation and lead counsel for the coalition, stated that "the interim congressional redistricting plan complies with the mandates of the Voting Rights Act by creating two additional Latino-majority congressional districts. Therefore, this litigation has achieved what the state of Texas failed to include in its legislatively enacted congressional redistricting plan—districts that recognize the significant population growth of Latinos in Texas."[6]

Drawing as they do on social science, history, legal cases, and political analysis, these ten rules will help provide a more complete map for understanding redistricting processes and outcomes.

Notes

Introduction

1. Nathaniel Persily, "Forty Years in the Political Thicket: Judicial Review of the Redistricting Process Since Reynolds v. Sims," in *Party Lines: Competition, Partisanship, and Congressional Redistricting,* Thomas E. Mann and Bruce E. Cain, eds., (Washington, DC: Brookings Institution, 2005).

2. Jonathan Winburn, *The Realities of Redistricting: Following the Rules and Limiting Gerrymandering in State Legislative Redistricting* (Lanham, MD: Lexington, 2008), 133.

3. National Conference of State Legislatures (NCSL), *Redistricting Law 2010* (Washington, DC: NCSL, 2009), 124–125.

4. J. Gerald Hebert, Paul M. Smith, Martina E. Vandenberg, and Michael B. DeSanctis, *The Realist's Guide to Redistricting: Avoiding the Legal Pitfalls* 2nd ed. (Chicago: American Bar Association, 2010).

5. Nina Perales, Luis Figueroa, and Criselda G. Rivas, "Voting Rights in Texas: 1982–2006," *Review of Law and Social Justice* 17 (2) (2008), 713–759.

6. Seth McKee and Daron K. Shaw, "Redistricting in Texas: Institutionalizing Republican Ascendancy," in *Redistricting in the New Millennium,* ed. Peter F. Galderisi (Lanham, MD: Lexington, 2005); Seth McKee and Brian K. Arbour, "Cracking Back: The Effectiveness of Partisan Redistricting in the Texas House of Representatives," *American Review of Politics* 26 (Winter 2006), 385–403; Seth McKee, Jeremy M. Teigen, and Matthew Turgeon, "The Partisan Impact of Congressional Redistricting: The Case of Texas, 2001–2003," *Social Science Quarterly* 87 (2006), 308–317; Danny Hayes and Seth McKee, "The Participa-

tory Effects of Redistricting," *American Journal of Political Science* 53 (4) (2009), 1006–1023; M. V. Hood, III, and Seth McKee, "Stranger Danger: Redistricting, Incumbent Recognition, and Vote Choice," *Social Science Quarterly* 91 (2) (2010), 344–358.

7. See Andrew Hacker, *Congressional Districting: The Issue of Equal Representation* (Washington, DC: Brookings Institution, 1963).

8. Wesley S. Chumlea, "The Politics of Legislative Apportionment in Texas 1921–1957," (PhD diss., University of Texas, 1959), 3–4; Ronald G. Claunch, Wesley S. Chumlea, and James G. Dickson, Jr., "Texas," in *Reapportionment Politics: The History of Redistricting in the 50 States*, Leroy Hardy, Alan Heslop, and Stuart Anderson, eds., (Beverly Hills, CA: Sage, 1981), 311.

9. Quoted in Chumlea, "The Politics of Legislative Apportionment in Texas," 88 and 92.

10. James R. Jensen, "Legislative Apportionment in Texas," *University of Houston Social Studies* Vol. 2 (Houston: University of Houston Public Affairs Research Center, 1964), 129.

11. Jensen, "Legislative Apportionment in Texas," 141.

12. Steve Bickerstaff, "Redistricting Texas: The History and Principles of Drawing Congressional and State Legislative Districts in Texas (1845–2010)," (Austin: University of Texas School of Law, 2011), 19.

13. The Legislative Redistricting Board is composed of the House Speaker, Senate president (i.e., lieutenant governor), attorney general, comptroller, and land commissioner.

14. Chumlea, "The Politics of Legislative Apportionment in Texas," 219–220.

15. Chandler Davidson, *Biracial Politics: Conflict and Coalition in the Metropolitan South* (Baton Rouge, LA: Louisiana University Press, 1972), 60; Davidson, *Minority Vote Dilution* (Washington, D.C.: Howard University Press, 1984).

16. Jensen, "Legislative Apportionment in Texas," 153.

17. See Steve Bickerstaff, *Lines in the Sand: Congressional Redistricting in Texas and the Downfall of Tom DeLay* (Austin: University of Texas Press, 2007), 412n.6.

18. In 1964, the Supreme Court would mandate a one person, one vote standard applicable to state and congressional districts.

19. Jensen, "Legislative Apportionment in Texas," 169.

20. *Houston Chronicle*, Oct. 20, 1963.

21. Bickerstaff, *Lines in the Sand*, 27.

22. Charles L. Zelden, *Voting Rights on Trial: A Handbook with Cases, Laws, and Documents* (Santa Barbara, CA: ABC-CLIO, 2002), Ch. 3; Abram Chayes, "The Role of the Judge in Public Law Litigation," *Harvard Law Review* 89 (1976), 1281–1316.

23. *Colegrove v. Green*, 328 U.S. 549 (1946).

24. Bernard Grofman, *Voting Rights, Voting Wrongs: The Legacy of Baker v. Carr* (New York: Priority, 1990), 3. See also Gordon E. Baker, *The Reapportionment Revolution: Representation, Political Power, and the Supreme Court* (New York: Random House, 1966).

25. *Baker v. Carr*, 369 U.S. 186 (1962).

26. Royce Hanson, *The Political Thicket: Reapportionment and Constitutional Democracy* (Englewood Cliffs, NJ, 1966).

27. *Gray v. Sanders*, 372 U.S. 368 (1963).

28. *Wesberry v. Sanders*, 376 U.S. 1 (1964).

29. *Reynolds v. Sims*, 377 U.S. 533 (1964).

30. See, for instance, Gordon Baker, *The Reapportionment Revolution*, 134–138.

31. E. E. Schattschneider, *The Semisovereign People: A Realist's View of Democracy in America* (New York: Holt, Rinehart and Winston, 1960), quotation at 8.

Chapter One

1. "Solons Denounce Connally's Stand on Redistricting," *Houston Chronicle*, October 23, 1963.

2. Ibid.

3. *House Journal*, 1965, 84.

4. Jerry D. Stephens, "A Case Study of Legislative Reapportionment in Texas 1961-1966," (MA thesis, University of Texas, 1966), 71.

5. For a summary of the growth of the Harris County Republicans and George Bush's role in that growth, see Robert A. Mosbacher, Sr., *Going to Windward, A Mosbacher Family Memoir* (College Station, TX: Texas A&M Press, 2010).

6. Bob Tutt, "State Reapportionment to be Pushed in Texas," *Houston Chronicle*, June 16, 1964, 15.

7. Because county lines could not be crossed, when a county had excess population it would be combined with an adjoining rural county or counties to create multicounty, multimember (flotorial) districts.

8. This material draws on my earlier work. See Gary A. Keith, *Eckhardt: There Once was a Congressman from Texas* (Austin: University of Texas Press, 2007), 192–194.

9. Texas Legislative Council, "Congressional Redistricting," Report No. 58-52, 1964.

10. *Houston Chronicle*, January 26, 1965.

11. Council report in Harris County Democratic Party Collection, "Harris County Election Analysis," Box 4C516.

12. Council report in Harris County Democratic Party Collection, "Harris County Plan," Box 4C516.

13. "Harris Legislators Show Mixed Reaction to Districting Proposal," *Houston Chronicle*, January 12, 1965, 21.

14. "Redistricting issue brings odd alliance: Eckhardt, GOP favor same plan," *Houston Tribune*, February 18, 1965, 1.

15. Stephens, "A Case Study," 59.

16. See Luther Hagard, Jr., August Spain, and Samuel Hamlett, "Legislative Redistricting in Texas," (Dallas: Southern Methodist University Arnold Foundation, 1965); Stephens, "A Case Study," 37–46.

17. "Rep. Floyd Unhappy with Plan Dividing Harris into Five Districts," *Houston Chronicle*, April 7, 1965.

18. Mickey Herskowitz, *Sharpstown Revisited: Frank Sharp and a Tale of Dirty Politics in Texas* (Austin: Eakin Press, 1994), 145.

19. Eventually, one African American, one Mexican American, and four Anglos won the state House seats from within Eckhardt's 8th congressional district (Curtis Graves, Lauro Cruz; Joe Allen, Lindon Williams, Glenn Vickery, and Rex Braun, respectively).

20. *Texas Observer*, June 11, 1965, 8.

21. Keith, *Eckhardt*, 104.

22. Handwritten note from Harris County Democratic Party Collection, Box 4C513.

23. "House Stamps OK on Districting Proposal," *Houston Chronicle*, May 6, 1965.

24. "Redistricting Errors Face Legislators," *Houston Chronicle*, May 31, 1965.

25. *Houston Chronicle*, May 30, 1965.

26. Institute of Public Affairs, "The Fifty-Ninth Texas Legislature: A Review of its Work," (Austin: University of Texas, 1966), 5–6.

27. Robert Brischetto, David R. Richards, Chandler Davidson, and Bernard Grofman, "Texas," in *Quiet Revolution in the South*, Chandler Davidson and Bernard Grofman, eds., (Princeton, NJ: Princeton University Press, 1994), 244.

28. Stephens, "A Case Study," 67.

29. *Bush v. Martin*, 251 F. Supp. 484 (S.D. Tex., 1966).

30. See James R. Jensen, "Legislative Apportionment in Texas," (Houston: University of Houston Social Studies Vol. 2, Public Affairs Research Center, 1964), 40–43; Stephens, "A Case Study," 64–67.

31. Steve Bickerstaff, "Redistricting Texas: The History and Principles of Drawing Congressional and State Legislative Districts in Texas (1845–2010)," (Austin: University of Texas School of Law, 2011), 24.

32. John Knaggs, *Austin American-Statesman*, October 8, 1994.

33. Chandler Davidson, *Biracial Politics: Conflict and Coalition in the*

Metropolitan South (Baton Rouge: Louisiana University Press, 1972), 69, 71; Dennis Simon, "Texans in the United States House of Representatives: A History of Electoral, Partisan, and Ideological Change, 1936–2000," (paper presented at the Jim Wright Symposium on Texas Congressional Leaders, Texas Christian University, Fort Worth, Texas, 2002).

34. Chandler Davidson, *Biracial Politics*, 97–98.

35. The only Texans in the House to vote for the Civil Rights Act were Albert Thomas, Jack Brooks, Henry B. González, and Jake Pickle.

36. Davidson, *Biracial Politics*, 97–98.

37. Richard Scammon, *America Votes* (Washington, D.C.: Congressional Quarterly Weekly, 1966).

38. Keith, *Eckhardt*, 199.

39. Sam Kinch, Jr., and Ben Procter, *Texas under a Cloud* (Austin: Jenkins, 1972).

40. William C. Adams, "The Introduction of Single-Member House Districts in Harris, Dallas, and Bexar Counties: Some Implications for Texas Politics," (paper presented at the Southwestern Political Science Association convention, Dallas, Texas, 1973), 2–7.

41. William C. Adams, "Redistricting the Texas House of Representatives, 1971–1972: A Case Study in the Politics and Law of Reapportionment," (MA thesis, Baylor University, 1972); David R. Richards, *Once Upon a Time in Texas: A Liberal in the Lone Star State* (Austin: University of Texas Press, 2002).

42. *Houston Post*, January 23, 1972.

43. Texas Legislative Council "Overview of Texas Redistricting," 2010.

44. Brischetto et al., "Texas," Ch. 8; Nina Perales, Luis Figueroa, and Criselda G. Rivas; "Voting Rights in Texas: 1982–2006," *Review of Law and Social Justice* 17 (2) (2008).

45. Steve Bickerstaff, *Lines in the Sand: Congressional Redistricting in Texas and the Downfall of Tom DeLay* (Austin: University of Texas Press, 2007).

Chapter Two

1. See, for instance, Congressman John Lewis's May 9, 2012, congressional speech on the bean-counting practice, reported at http://thinkprogress.org/justice/2012/05/10/482210/rep-paul-broun-tries-to-defund-voting-rights-act/. See also J. Morgan Kousser, *The Shaping of Southern Politics: Suffrage Restriction and the Establishment of the One-Party South, 1880–1910* (New Haven: Yale University Press), 1974.

2. For account of the Wheeler Street riot, see George Lipsitz, *How Racism Takes Place* (Philadelphia: Temple University Press, 2011), 156–157 and Yolanda Braxton, "Bricks Without Straw—The almost forgotten 40 year history of the Tigerwalk," *TSU Herald*, August 31, 2007. See also Dwight David Watson, "From Smoke to Fire: Causes of the 1967 Texas Southern University Riot" (paper presented at the Texas State Historical Association Meeting in San Antonio, March 1995).

3. *Kilgarlin v. Martin*, 252 F. Supp. 404 (S.D. Tex. 1966); *Graves v. Barnes*, 343 F. Supp. 704 (W.D. Tex. 1972).

4. See Gary Keith, *Eckhardt: There Once was a Congressman from Texas* (Austin: University of Texas Press, 2007), 228.

5. *Moses v. City of Houston*, Cause No. H-75-1731 (S.D. Tex. 1973).

6. *Greater Houston Civic Council v. Mann*, 440 F. Supp. 696 (S.D. Tex. 1977).

7. Art. 2774b, V.T.C.S., from HB 313 (*General and Special Laws of Texas, 64th Regular Session, Vol. 2* Ch. 717, 2300–2301 (1975).

8. "Best Little Statehouse in Texas," CBS Reports, New York: CBS News, August 26, 1981.

9. Molly Ivins, "TV: 'CBS Reports' Views Texas Legislature," *New York Times*, August 26, 1981.

10. By longstanding custom, the House did not do any work on a Senate redistricting plan, nor did the Senate work on a House redistricting plan. The legislative norm is that the House simply accepts the work of the Senate on its own district lines, and vice versa.

11. Ultimately, Clements's plan for Congress passed but was declared to be a racial gerrymander and thrown out in *Terrazas v. Clements*, 537 F. Supp. 514 (N.D. Tex. 1982).

12. See HB 960 Bill Analysis, *House Study Group Daily Floor Report*, May 27, 1981.

13. *Bush v. Vera*, 116 S. Ct. 1941 (1996).

Chapter Three

1. *Craddick v. Smith*, 471 S.W. 2d 375 (Tex. 1971).

2. *Mauzy v. Redistricting Board*, 471 S.W. 2d 570, 573 (Tex. 1971).

3. *Graves v. Barnes*, 343 F. Supp. 704 (W.D Tex. 1972).

4. *White v. Regester*, 412 U.S. 755 (1973).

5. *White v. Weiser*, 412 U.S. 783 (1973).

6. *Kirkpatrick v. Preisler*, 394 U.S. 526 (1969)

7. *Clements v. Valles*, 620 S.W. 2d 112 (1981).

8. *Seamon v. Upham*, 456 U.S. 37 (1982).

9. *Terrazas v. Clements*, 537 F. Supp. 514 (1982).

10. *Terrazas v. Clements*, 581 F. Supp. 1319 (1983).

11. *Terrazas v. Clements*, 581 F. Supp. 1325 (1984).

12. *Mena v. Richards*, Cause No. C-454-91-F (332nd Dist. Ct., Hidalgo Co.) (1991); *Quiroz v. Richards*, Cause No. C-4395-91-F (332nd Dist. Ct., Hidalgo Co.) (1991).

13. *Terrazas v. Ramirez*, 829 S.W. 2d 712 (Tex. 1991).

14. *Terrazas v. Slagle*, 789 F. Supp. 828 (W.D. Tex. 1991).

15. *Bush v. Vera*, 116 S.Ct. 1941 (1996).

16. *Armbrister v. Morales*, 943 S.W. 2d 202 (Austin Court of Appeals 1997).

17. See Steve Bickerstaff, *Lines in the Sand: Congressional Redistricting in Texas and the Downfall of Tom DeLay* (Austin: University of Texas Press, 2007).

18. *Balderas v. State of Texas*, no. 6:01-CV-158, slip op. (E.D. Tex. 2004).

19. *Perry v. Del Rio*, 67 S.W. 3d (Tex. 2001).

20. *LULAC v. Perry*, 548 U.S. 399 (2006).

Chapter Four

1. See Liberal Arts Instructional Technology Services of the University of Texas, "The Partisan Composition of the Texas Legislature," http://www.laits.utexas.edu/txp_media/html/leg/features/0303_01/slide1.html and http://www.laits.utexas.edu/txp_media/html/leg/features/0303_01/slide2.html.

2. *Mena v. Richards*, No. C-454–91-F, 332nd District Court, Hidalgo Co. (1991); *Mena v. Mosbacher*, No. C-B-91–010, U.S. District Court, S.D. Tex. (1991).

3. See Texas Legislative Council, "1990s Redistricting Chronology," http://www.tlc.state.tx.us/redist/chron_1990.htm. See also House Research Organization, "Redistricting for the Nineties: A Progress Report," Special Legislative Report No. 175, Feb. 28, 1992.

4. The cases were filed under civil action numbers A-91-CA-425, A-91-CA-426, and A-91-CA-428, in the U.S. District Court for the Western District of Texas, Austin Division. Bob Slagle, the lead defendant, was the chairman of the Texas Democratic Party.

5. *Terrazas v. Slagle*, 789 F. Supp. 828, 830 (W.D. Tex. 1991).

6. The same thing happened in 2011, when Texas again sought preclearance from the D.C. District Court rather than from President Obama's Department of Justice.

7. No. C-4395–91-F, 332nd Judicial District, Hidalgo County, Texas.

8. See generally *Terrazas v. Ramirez*, 829 S.W. 2d 712, 714–715 (Tex. 1991).

9. *Terrazas v. Ramirez*, 829 S.W. 2d at 715–716.

10. The nineteen senators who approved the Senate "settlement plan" were all Democrats, and the plan plainly favored their party. The House plan also favored the Democrats.

11. *Terrazas v. Ramirez*, 829 S.W. 2d at 717.

12. *Terrazas v. Ramirez*, 829 S.W. at 713.

13. *Terrazas v. Ramirez*, 829 S.W. 2d at 718. This holding played a role in the redistricting battle after the 2000 census.

14. *Terrazas v. Ramirez*, 829 S.W. 2d at 719–723.

15. *Terrazas v. Ramirez*, 829 S.W. 2d at 726.

16. This hearing began on December 10, 1991.

17. *Terrazas v. Slagle*, 789 F. Supp. 828 (W.D. Tex. 1991) (three-judge court).

18. See Texas Legislative Council, "1990s Redistricting," http://www.tlc.state.tx.us/redist/history_1990.html.

19. See House Research Organization, "Redistricting for the Nineties: A Progress Report," Special Legislative Report No. 175, Feb. 28, 1992, 16.

20. See Rule 5.14, Texas Senate Rules.

21. The court's plan had a lesser effect on the partisan composition of the House.

22. Secretary Hannah's directive is set forth verbatim in *Terrazas v. Slagle*, 821 F. Supp. 1154, 1158 n.4 (W.D. Tex. 1992) (three-judge court).

23. *Terrazas v. Slagle*, 821 F. Supp. at 1158.

24. *Terrazas v. Slagle*, 821 F. Supp. at 1161.

25. Ripeness is a legal principle under which a suit does not properly invoke a court's jurisdiction unless it is based on existing facts that give rise to a concrete dispute. A suit filed before a controversy becomes ripe does not establish dominant jurisdiction.

26. *Associated Republicans of Texas v. Cuellar*, No. 2001-26894, 281st District Court, Harris County, Texas.

27. *Cotera v. Perry*, Cause No. GN-101660, 353rd District Court, Travis County, Texas. Filed May 31, 2001.

28. *Rivas v. Cuellar*, Cause No. 2001-33760, 152nd District Court, Harris County, Texas. This case later was consolidated with the *Associated Republicans* case in the 281st District Court.

29. *Connolly v. Perry*, Cause No. GN-102250, in the 98th District Court, Travis County, Texas.

30. The cases in the Eastern District, which were filed in Tyler, were styled *Balderas v. Texas*, *Mayfield v. Texas*, and *Manley v. Texas*. The Western District cases were styled *Associated Republicans of Texas v. Texas* and *Anderson v. Texas*.

31. Judge Hannah, the former Texas secretary of state who played a

large role in the 1990s redistricting battles, had since been appointed to the federal bench by President Clinton.

32. *Manley v. Texas*, U.S. Dist. LEXIS 25427, *9-*10 (E.D. Tex. July 20, 2001). The July 20 opinion memorialized rulings that the panel had announced in open court at a hearing on July 6.

33. *Manley v. Texas*, U.S. Dist. LEXIS 25427, *9-*10 (E.D. Tex. 2001).

34. *Del Rio v. Perry*, 66 S.W. 2d at 239 (Tex. 2001).

35. *Del Rio v. Perry*, 66 S.W. 2d at 256.

36. *Del Rio v. Perry*, 66 S.W. 2d at 256.

37. At trial, State Representative Ron Wilson, an African American from the Houston area, testified in support of Republican-backed plans. He did so, he said, because he was tired of the Democrats' use of minority voters as "cannon fodder" in plans drawn to protect Anglo Democrats, not to elect minority candidates. Some of the plans presented by Republican interests would have enhanced the likelihood that an African American could be elected to Congress from the Houston area.

38. *Perry v. Del Rio*, 67 S.W. 3d at 85, 88.

39. *Perry v. Del Rio*, 67 S.W. 3d at 89.

40. *Perry v. Del Rio*, 67 S.W. 3d at 94.

41. *Perry v. Del Rio*, 67 S.W. 3d at 94.

42. *Perry v. Del Rio*, 67 S.W. 3d at 95.

Chapter Five

1. See David Montejano, *Anglos and Mexican Americans in the Making of Texas, 1836–1986* (Austin: University of Texas Press, 1987), 288–297; Robert Brischetto, David R. Richards, Chandler Davidson, and Bernard Grofman, "Texas," in *Quiet Revolution in the South: Impact of the Voting Rights Act, 1965–1990*, Chandler Davidson and Bernard Grofman, eds., (Princeton, NJ: Princeton University Press, 1994), 235–242.

2. See Montejano, *Anglos and Mexican Americans*, 292–293; see Brischetto, "Texas," 254–257.

3. See Montejano, *Anglos and Mexican Americans*; see Brischetto, "Texas."

4. Brischetto, "Texas," 293.

5. Steve Bickerstaff, "Reapportionment by State Legislatures: A Guide for the 1980s," *Southwestern Law Journal* 34 (607) (1984), 633–634.

6. Montejano, "Texas," 293.

7. *Baker v. Carr*, 369 U.S. 186, 208–209 (1962).

8. *Reynolds v. Sims*, 377 U.S. 533, 568 (1964).

9. *Reynolds v. Sims*, at 554–556.

10. *Reynolds v. Sims*, at 555.

11. James Blacksher and Larry T. Menefee, "From Reynolds v. Sims to City of Mobile v. Bolden: Have the White Suburbs Commandeered the Fifteenth Amendment?" *Hastings Law Journal* 34 (1982), 1.

12. Blackshear and Menefee, "From Reynolds v. Sims to City of Mobile," 1.

13. See *Kilgarlin v. Hill*, 386 U.S. 120, 121 (1967) affirming without discussion the district court's rejection of claims by Black Texas voters that the state's legislative redistricting plan was a racial gerrymander and that the multimember districts diluted Black voting strength; *Whitcomb v. Chavis*, 403 U.S. 124, 141–155 (1971) recognizing that multimember districts could have the effect of submerging Black voting strength, but the court's majority could not agree that the record contained sufficient proof of constitutionally impermissible dilution of Black voting strength in Indianapolis.

14. *White v. Regester*, 412 U.S. 755 (1973).

15. *White v. Regester*, 765–766.

16. *White v. Regester*, 765–766.

17. *White v. Regester*, 766–770.

18. *Zimmer v. McKeithen*, 485 F. 2d 1297 (5th Cir. 1973) (en banc), aff'd sub nom. *East Carroll Parish Sch. Bd. v. Marshall*, 424 U.S. 636 (1976).

19. *Zimmer v. McKeithen*, at 1305.

20. Ibid.

21. Anti-single-shot provisions include such things as the place system or rules that prohibit a voter from casting less than his/her full allotment of votes in a particular election.

22. See *Zimmer v. McKeithen*, at 1305.

23. See Bickerstaff, "Reapportionment by State Legislatures," 326–333.

24. *City of Mobile v. Bolden*, 446 U.S. 55, 66 (1980).

25. *City of Mobile v. Bolden*, 66.

26. Southwestern Reporter No. 97-417, at 2 (1982) reprinted in 1982 U.S.C.C.A.N. 177, at 206–207.

27. Southwestern Reporter No. 97-417, at 2 (1982) reprinted in 1982 U.S.C.C.A.N. 177, at 205–207.

28. Southwestern Reporter No. 97-417, at 2 (1982) reprinted in 1982 U.S.C.C.A.N. 177, at 193.

29. Southwestern Reporter No. 97-417, at 2 (1982) reprinted in 1982 U.S.C.C.A.N. 177, at 207.

30. Southwestern Reporter No. 97-417, at 2 (1982) reprinted in 1982 U.S.C.C.A.N. 177, at 207.

31. *Thornburg v. Gingles*, 478 U.S. 30 (1986).

32. *Thornburg v. Gingles*, 47–51.

33. *Thornburg v. Gingles*, at 48 n. 15.

34. *Thornburg v. Gingles*, 50–51.

35. For a look at the battles over at-large districts in Texas cities and school districts, see J. L. Polinard, Robert D. Wrinkle, Tomas Longoria, and Norman E. Binder, *Electoral Structure and Urban Policy: the Impact on Mexican American Communities* (Armonk, N.Y.: M. E. Sharpe, 1994).

36. Now renamed Texas Rio Grande Legal Aid (TRLA).

37. See Brischetto et al., "Texas," 254–257 and Montejano, *Anglos and Mexican Americans*, 292–293.

38. *Findings of Fact and Conclusions of Law*, at 23–26, *Alonzo v. Jones* (S.D. Tex. 1983) (No. C-81-227).

39. *Alonzo v. Jones* 7.

40. *Alonzo v. Jones* 7.

41. See Brischetto et al., "Texas," 254–255.

42. For current and historical MALDEF voting rights and redistricting initiatives, see http://maldef.org/voting_rights/litigation/index.html and http://maldef.org/redistricting/index.html.

43. See *Texas State Directory* (Austin, TX: Texas State Directory Press, 1994), 291–445.

44. See Bickerstaff, "Reapportionment by State Legislatures," 633–634; Brischetto, "Texas," 235–236.

45. See Brischetto et al., "Texas," 254–260.

46. *Reyes v. City of Farmers Branch*, 586 F. 3rd 1019 (5th Cir. 2009).

47. See James Madison's Federalist No. 57, *The Federalist Papers*, ed. Clinton Rossiter (New York: New American Library, 1961), 351: "Who are to be the electors of the federal representatives? Not the rich, more than the poor; not the learned, more than the ignorant; not the haughty heirs of distinguished names, more than the humble sons of obscure and unpropitious fortune. The electors are to be the great body of the people of the United States."

Chapter Six

1. Placing the word "political" in quotes reflects the title of the recent book by Charles Bullock, *Redistricting: The Most Political Activity in America* (Lanham, MD: Rowman & Littlefield, 2010).

2. V. O. Key, Jr., *Southern Politics in State and Nation* (New York: Vintage Books, 1949), 254.

3. We adopt the most common definition of the South: the eleven ex-Confederate states of Alabama, Arkansas, Florida, Georgia, Louisiana, Mississippi, North Carolina, South Carolina, Tennessee, Texas, and Virginia. See Joseph A. Aistrup, *The Southern Strategy Revisited: Republi-*

can Top-Down Advancement in the South (Lexington: University Press of Kentucky, 1996).

4. See Earl Black and Merle Black, *The Rise of Southern Republicans* (Cambridge, MA: Harvard University Press, 2002); for more details on the 1992 Texas congressional map see also Michael Barone and Grant Ujifusa, *The Almanac of American Politics 1994* (Washington, D.C.: National Journal, 1993).

5. This figure is based on the voting age population. The converse of this number (an 82 percent redrawn voting age population) is displayed in Table 6.1.

6. In the 1996 case *Bush v. Vera*, Texas had to alter the lines in 13 of its 30 congressional districts because the Court ruled that the 1992 map was an unconstitutional racial gerrymander (see Katharine Inglis Butler, "Redistricting in a Post-Shaw Era: A Small Treatise Accompanied By Districting Guidelines for Legislators, Litigants, and Courts," *University of Richmond Law Review* 36 (1) (2002), 137–270.

7. On this point see Seth C. McKee, *Republican Ascendancy in Southern U.S. House Elections* (Boulder, CO: Westview Press, 2010).

8. There is little question that Republicans were victorious in Districts 23 and 27—both majority Hispanic districts—only because of low Hispanic turnout. In District 23, Republican Francisco Canseco bested incumbent Democrat Ciro Rodriguez by 7,505 votes and in District 27, Republican Blake Farenthold took 775 more votes than Democratic Representative Solomon Ortiz. (Data are from the Texas Secretary of State.)

9. Data are from Michael Barone, Richard E. Cohen, and Grant Ujifusa, *The Almanac of American Politics 2002* (Washington, D.C.: National Journal, 2001).

10. *Balderas v. Texas* (2001).

11. *Growe v. Emison*, 507 U.S. 25 (1993). See also *Perry v. Del Rio*, 67 S.W. 3rd (Tex. 2001). Not all the Republicans on the state Supreme Court agreed with the decision to vacate the trial judge's plan.

12. Even the U.S. Supreme Court in *LULAC v. Perry* (2006) acknowledged that the Democratic gerrymander was left more or less undisturbed. See also Ronald Keith Gaddie, "The Texas Redistricting, Measure for Measure," *Extensions*, Fall 2004, 19. Available at http://www.ou.edu/special/albertctr/extensions/fall2004/Gaddie.html.

13. More precisely, Republicans won 54.9 percent of the Texas congressional votes in 2002, as referenced in Gaddie, "The Texas Redistricting, Measure for Measure."

14. For further details on the 2003 Texas redistricting battle, see Steve Bickerstaff, *Lines in the Sand: Congressional Redistricting in Texas and the Downfall of Tom DeLay* (Austin: University of Texas Press, 2007);

Seth C. McKee, Jeremy M. Teigen, and Mathieu Turgeon, "The Partisan Impact of Congressional Redistricting: The Case of Texas, 2001–2003," *Social Science Quarterly* 87 (2) 2006, 308–317; Seth C. McKee and Daron R. Shaw, "Redistricting in Texas: Institutionalizing Republican Ascendancy," in *Redistricting in the New Millennium*, ed. Peter F. Galderisi (Lanham, MD: Lexington Books, 2005).

15. In fact, Judge Rosenthal, though appointed by a Republican president, identifies herself as an independent.

16. Butler, "Redistricting in a Post-Shaw Era"; Adam B. Cox and Thomas J. Miles, "Judging the Voting Rights Act," *Columbia Law Review* 108 (2008), 1–54; Mark J. McKenzie, "The Influence of Partisanship, Ideology, and the Law on Redistricting Decisions in the Federal Courts." *Political Research Quarterly* 65 (4): 799–813.

17. *Thornburg v. Gingles*, 478 U.S. 30 (1986).

18. Ambiguity in VRA precedent allows federal judges to further their own ideological or partisan interests (see McKenzie, "The Influence of Partisanship, Ideology, and the Law on Redistricting Decisions in the Federal Courts"). Sometimes judges use this ambiguity to rule in favor of their own party's redistricting plans. At other times, judges employ their own ideological conceptions of the law in VRA cases, regardless of whether their ideological predispositions would help out their own political party or not. For instance, Republican-appointed judges are less likely to find evidence of state discrimination in drawing electoral lines when compared to their Democratic colleagues. It is difficult to disentangle these explanations with respect to what went on in Texas's lower federal courts in the 2000s. The behavior of the judges in these federal trial courts could be explained away as either partisan attempts to help their own political party or as principled differences based on conservative or liberal interpretations of VRA law.

19. As stated earlier, one of the three threshold inquiries into VRA violations asks whether the minority population is compact enough to straightforwardly comprise a majority-minority district. In complying with the VRA, a state is not under any obligation to connect minority populations in faraway locales. On the contrary, if the state were to do so, it could expose itself to litigation under *Shaw v. Reno* (1993) claims of racial gerrymandering, contravening the 14th Amendment's Equal Protection clause.

20. It matters little in VRA jurisprudence that Bonilla himself was Hispanic.

21. Like VRA jurisprudence, the Supreme Court precedents in partisan gerrymandering and the legal standard set by *Davis v. Bandemer* (1986) are quite murky. However, unlike VRA jurisprudence, the standards for partisan gerrymandering claims appear so ambiguous and the

bar set for a violation appears so high that few federal courts have ever found evidence of an unconstitutional partisan gerrymander.

22. See *Henderson v. Perry*, 399 F. Supp. 2d. 756 (2005). Judge Ward lamented in his concurrence and dissent in the *Session v. Perry* (2004) case that past partisan gerrymandering precedent did not provide him with adequate authority to strike down the Republican plan as an unconstitutional partisan gerrymander. When the U.S. Supreme Court remanded the case for the lower court to consider their decision a second time in light of the *Vieth* case, Judge Ward adhered to his previous reasoning and again struck down the partisan gerrymandering claims of plaintiffs.

23. See *LULAC v. Perry*, 548 U.S. 399, 435 (2006).

24. See *LULAC v. Perry*, 548 U.S. 399, 442 (2006).

25. *LULAC v. Perry*, 457 F. Supp. 2d 716 (2006).

26. Richard F. Fenno, Jr., *Home Style: House Members in Their Districts* (Boston, MA: Little Brown, 1978).

27. Robert S. Erikson and Gerald C. Wright, "Voters, Candidates, and Issues in Congressional Elections," in *Congress Reconsidered*, Lawrence C. Dodd and Bruce I. Oppenheimer, eds. (Washington, D.C.: CQ Press, 2009).

28. See Black and Black, *The Rise of Southern Republicans*; James E. Campbell, "The Presidential Pulse and the 1994 Midterm Congressional Election," *Journal of Politics* 59 (3) (1997), 830–857; Gary C. Jacobson, "Reversal of Fortune: The Transformation of U.S. House Elections in the 1990s," in *Continuity and Change in House Elections*, David W. Brady, John F. Cogan, and Morris P. Fiorina, eds. (Stanford, CA: Stanford University Press, 2000); Jeffrey M. Stonecash, *Reassessing the Incumbency Effect* (New York: Cambridge University Press, 2008).

29. It also helped that most Democrats avoided facing strong Republican challengers and often any Republican opponent. See Gary C. Jacobson, *The Electoral Origins of Divided Government: Competition in U.S. House Elections, 1946–1988* (Boulder, CO: Westview Press, 1990); "Reversal of Fortune"; and *The Politics of Congressional Elections* (New York: Pearson Longman, 2009).

30. See Danny Hayes and Seth C. McKee, "The Participatory Effects of Redistricting," *American Journal of Political Science* 53 (4) (2009), 1006–1023; McKee, "Redistricting and Familiarity with U.S. House Candidates," *American Politics Research* 36 (6) (2008), 962–979. As a stark example of this behavior, one of the authors of this chapter interviewed a federal judge overseeing redistricting litigation who said he had no idea who his congressman was until he went to the polls because, he said, of the splitting of precincts and the fact that the lines changed back and forth a few times in his state.

31. See M. V. Hood, III, and Seth C. McKee, "Stranger Danger: Re-

districting, Incumbent Recognition, and Vote Choice," *Social Science Quarterly* 91 (2) (2010), 344–358.

32. This point is emphasized in the work of Scott W. Desposato and John R. Petrocik, "The Variable Incumbency Advantage: New Voters, Redistricting, and the Personal Vote," *American Journal of Political Science* 47 (1) (2003), 18–32; "Redistricting and Incumbency: The New Voter Effect," in *Redistricting in the New Millennium*, ed. Peter F. Galderisi (Lanham, MD: Lexington Books, 2005), 35–63; but see also Robert G. Boatright, who finds that incumbents will expend energy acquainting themselves with redrawn constituents if they know in advance what the newly drawn sections of their altered districts will be, in "Static Ambition in a Changing World: Legislators' Preparations for, and Responses to, Redistricting," *State Politics & Policy Quarterly* 4 (4) (2004), 436–454.

33. See McKee, *Republican Ascendancy in Southern U.S. House Elections*.

34. See Timothy Lynch, "Drawn to (not) Run: District Continuity and Quality Challengers," (paper presented at the annual meeting of the Southern Political Science Association, New Orleans, LA, 2011).

35. See Marc J. Hetherington, Bruce A. Larson, and Suzanne Globbeti, "The Redistricting Cycle and Strategic Candidate Decisions in U.S. House Races," *Journal of Politics* 65 (4) (2003), 1221–1235.

36. This point is made by John R. Petrocik and Scott W. Desposato, "Incumbency and Short-Term Influences on Voters," *Political Research Quarterly* 57 (3) (2004), 363–373.

37. Stephen Ansolabehere, James M. Snyder, Jr., and Charles Stewart, III, contend that, in the long run, incumbents perform better among their old constituents because they have nurtured a successful home style with these more familiar constituents, in "Old Voters, New Voters, and the Personal Vote: Using Redistricting to Measure the Incumbency Advantage," *American Journal of Political Science* 44 (1) (2000), 17–34.

38. See Seth C. McKee, "The Effects of Redistricting on Voting Behavior in Incumbent U.S. House Elections, 1992–1994," *Political Research Quarterly* 61 (1) (2008), 122–133; *Republican Ascendancy in Southern U.S. House Elections*; Desposato and Petrocik, "The Variable Incumbency Advantage" and "Redistricting and Incumbency"; Petrocik and Desposato, "Incumbency and Short-Term Influences on Voters."

39. Kevin A. Hill and Nicol C. Rae, "What Happened to the Democrats in the South? U.S. House Elections, 1992–1996," *Party Politics* 6 (1) (2000), 5–22.

40. On this point see Antoine Yoshinaka and Chad Murphy, "Partisan Gerrymandering and Population Instability: Completing the Redistricting Puzzle," *Political Geography* 28 (8) (2009), 451–462.

41. The TLC is a nonpartisan state agency that performs technical work related to Texas redistricting.

42. This is the link to the TLC memo ("Voting Tabulation Districts") that describes the 2010 VTDs in greater detail: ftp://ftpgis1.tlc.state .tx.us/2011_Redistricting_Data/VTDs/Geography/ReadMe.txt.

43. In order to determine which VTDs were redrawn from 2002 through 2010, we had to start our overlay with the 2000 congressional map.

44. Or more precisely, the same incumbent since 2006 and until he or she no longer seeks reelection or is defeated.

45. By defining redrawn VTDs as those an incumbent receives as a direct consequence of redistricting, we are not concerned with an analysis of VTDs in open-seat contests (districts without an incumbent seeking reelection).

46. As we will show in Table 6.1, there are other redrawn VTDs that Doggett inherited in the 2004 election (26.6 percent of the district population came from District 15 and 24.3 percent of the district population came from District 28) and this accounts for the voting age percentage of redrawn constituents in District 25 in 2004 (61 percent).

47. Because of multiple redistrictings, it is possible to further refine the redrawn classification. Consider an incumbent who was first elected before 2000. In the 2004 election this incumbent might have some redrawn VTDs that were in the district of another incumbent for 2000 and 2002. The incumbent might have other redrawn VTDs that he represented in 2000 but were then drawn into another incumbent's district in 2002 only to return to the original incumbent in 2004 (we can call these "redrawn back" VTDs). Finally, the last type of redrawn VTD is one that was redrawn in consecutive elections. In this case, for incumbent A in 2004, the VTD was redrawn, but in 2002 it was redrawn into a different incumbent's district from the one it was in for the 2000 election (we can call these "redrawn different" VTDs). This can get even more complicated if we consider the example of an incumbent who was elected before 2000 and had his district redrawn in 2002, 2004, and 2006 (i.e., Lamar Smith in District 21). We do not include this delineation of the redrawn classification for our subsequent analyses mainly because the results are not much different, and there is a considerable reduction in the number of VTDs that fall under these designated subcategories of redrawn VTDs.

48. Few studies have engaged in this type of analysis, but one exception is Mark E. Rush, "Redistricting and Partisan Fluidity: Do We Really Know a Gerrymander When We See One?" *Political Geography* 19 (2000), 249–260.

49. The blank spaces in the table either mean that the incumbent was running in their initial contest as a candidate in an open seat (Cuellar in 2004, Hensarling in 2002, Neugebauer in a special election to re-

place Republican Larry Combest in 2003, Burgess in 2002, and Carter in 2002), or the incumbent retired (Turner in 2004), or the incumbent switched parties (Hall was no longer a Democrat in 2004), or the incumbent lost in a primary (Rodriguez in 2004), or the incumbent had no changes to their district in 2006 (in other words, the district was 0 percent redrawn in 2006).

50. In Texas, every Democratic and Republican incumbent won re-election in 2002.

51. In the 2004 presidential election, 70 percent of the two-party vote in District 17 went to Republican George W. Bush. Michael Barone, Richard E. Cohen, and Grant Ujifusa, *The Almanac of American Politics 2006* (Washington, D.C.: National Journal, 2005).

52. In District 28, Hispanic Democrat Ciro Rodriguez lost in the 2004 primary to Hispanic Henry Cuellar.

53. Black and Black (*The Rise of Southern Republicans*) define a 60 percent (or higher) share of the two-party vote as a landslide.

54. Because of the 2006 court-ordered redistricting that affected five Texas U.S. House districts, these contests were held as Louisiana-style open primaries. So, in 2006 it was possible to have multiple candidates with the same party label running in Districts 15, 21, 23, 25, and 28. Like Louisiana, if no candidate received a simple majority, then the initial special election would be followed by a special runoff. A special runoff—a contest that included six Democrats and one Independent—was only necessary in District 23 because Henry Bonilla failed to win a simple majority (48.6 percent of the total votes) in the first special election. In the VTD-based analyses for these five redrawn districts in 2006, if there was more than one major party challenger taking on the incumbent, then we calculated the two-party vote at the VTD level based on the votes won by the more successful challenger. In Districts 15 and 21, each incumbent faced two major party challengers: Republicans Paul B. Haring and Eddie Zamora challenged Democratic incumbent Ruben Hinojosa in District 15, and Democrats John Courage and Gene Kelly challenged Republican incumbent Lamar Smith in District 21. In these cases we computed the two-party vote for Haring and Courage because they won more votes than their co-partisans. We only computed the VTD-level vote returns for the special election runoff in District 23. There was only one Republican challenging Democrat Lloyd Doggett in District 25. A Democrat (Frank Enriquez) challenged Democrat Henry Cuellar in District 28, but since there was no Republican running, we deem the race uncontested.

55. In regression analysis, one of the four categories has to be omitted in order to run the model. The omitted category operates as the group to which all the other racial groups are compared to statistically.

56. In 2002, these VTDs were in the following congressional districts: District 3 (represented by Republican Sam Johnson), District 5 (an open seat won by Republican Jeb Hensarling), and District 30 (represented by Democrat Eddie Bernice Johnson). In 2002, Congressman Frost represented District 24 and Congressman Sessions represented District 32.

57. In the legal arena, see, for example, the important Supreme Court cases of *White v. Regester*, 412 U.S. 755 (1973) or *LULAC v. Perry*, 548 U.S. 399 (2006). Electorally, the Democratic gerrymander of 1991 and the Republican gerrymander of 2003 offer some of the most extreme and successful gerrymanders in modern times.

58. See, for example, Alan Abramowitz, Brad Alexander, and Matthew Gunning, "Drawing the Line on District Competition: A Rejoinder," *PS: Political Science & Politics* 39 (1) (2006), 95–97.

59. Sanford Levinson, "Symposium: Baker v. Carr: A Commemorative Symposium, Panel II: One Person, One Vote: A Theoretical and Practical Examination: One Person, One Vote: A Mantra in Need of Meaning," *North Carolina Law Review*, 80 (May 2002), 1269–1297.

60. Those supporting commission processes include groups such as the League of Women Voters and Common Cause (see, for example, http://www.commoncause.org/site/pp.asp?c=dkLNK1MQIwG&b=366007) as well as political scientists such as Herbert Asher (http://www.ohio citizen.org/moneypolitics/ron/ron.htm) and the late Donald Stokes, "Is There a Better Way to Redistrict?" in *Race and Redistricting in the 1990s*, ed. Bernard Grofman (New York: Agathon Press, 1998).

61. See Jeremy Buchman, *Drawing Lines in Quicksand: Courts, Legislatures, and Redistricting* (New York: Peter Lang Publishing, 2003). Mark J. McKenzie (2012) has found that federal courts are no more likely to uphold commission-drawn plans as legally valid when compared to plans drawn by a legislature. And Winburn (2008) has found that some state commissions, depending on how they are constructed, do a better job at creating politically neutral plans than other commissions.

62. See *Perry v. Perez*, Nos. 11-713, 11-714, 11-715 *Supreme Court of the United States.* January 20, 2012, per curiam; see also *Perez v. Texas*, Civil Action No. 11-CA-360-OLG-JES-XR (November 23, 2011 — U.S. Dist. Ct., W.D. Tex.).

Conclusion

1. U.S. Census Bureau, "State and County Quick Facts," http://quickfacts.census.gov/qfd/states/48000.html.

2. *Teuber et al. v. Texas et al.*, Cause No. 4:11-cv-0059 (U.S. Dist. Ct., E.D. Tex. 2011).

3. *Mexican American Legislative Caucus v. Texas*, No. C-902-11-C, 139th Judicial District, Hidalgo Co., Tex., 2011. The case was soon kicked over to the federal court in Hidalgo County.

4. *Perez and Dutton v. Texas*, No. 11-20238-CN, W.D. Tex.

5. *Mexican American Legislative Caucus v. Texas*, No. SA 11 CA 0361, W.D. Tex, 2011.

6. *Barton v. State of Texas*, No. 11-20238-CN, Navarro Co., Tex.

7. *Texas v. U.S.*, Document 106, 1:11-cv-01303-RMC-TBG-BAH, November 8, 2011.

8. *Texas v. U.S.*, District docket 11-1303.

Epilogue

1. Jonathan Winburn, *The Realities of Redistricting: Following the Rules and Limiting Gerrymandering in State Legislative Redistricting* (Lanham, MD: Lexington, 2008), 133.

2. *Bush v. Martin*, 251 F. Supp. 484 (S.D. Tex., 1966).

3. *White v. Weiser*, 412 U.S. 783 (1973).

4. *Seamon v. Upham*, 456 U.S. 37 (1982).

5. *Bush v. Vera*, 116 S.Ct. 1941 (1996).

6. Ross Ramsey, "Court Delivers Election Maps for Texas House, Congress," *Texas Tribune*, February 28, 2012, http://www.texastribune .org/texas-redistricting/redistricting/court-delivers-election-maps -texas-house-congress/.

Sources

Cases Cited

Alonzo v. Jones. 1983. No. C-81-227 (S.D. Tex.).
Anderson v. Texas. 2001. (W.D. Tex.).
Armbrister v. Morales. 1997. 943 S.W. 2d 202 (Austin Court of Appeals).
Associated Republicans of Texas v. Cuellar. 2001. Cause No. 2001-26894 (281st Dist. Ct., Harris Co., Tex.).
Associated Republicans of Texas v. Texas. 2001. (W.D. Tex.).
Baker v. Carr. 1962. 369 U.S. 186.
Balderas v. Texas. 2004. No. 6:01-CV-158, slip op. (E.D. Tex.).
Bush v. Martin. 1963. 224 F. Supp. 499 (S.D. Tex.).
Bush v. Martin. 1966. 251 F. Supp. 484 (S.D. Tex.).
Bush v. Vera. 1996. 116 S.Ct. 1941.
City of Mobile v. Bolden. 1980. 446 U.S. 55, 66.
Clements v. Valles. 1981. 620 S.W. 2d 112.
Colegrove v. Green. 1946. 328 U.S. 549.
Connolly v. Perry. 2001. Cause No. GN-102250 (98th Dist. Ct., Travis Co., Tex.).
Cotera v. Perry. 2001. Cause No. GN-101660 (353rd Dist. Ct., Travis Co., Tex.).
Craddick v. Smith. 1971. 471 S.W. 2d 375 (Tex.).
Davis v. Bandemer. 1986. 478 U.S. 109.
Del Rio v. Perry. 2001. 66 S.W. 2d 239 (Tex.).
East Carroll Parish Sch. Bd. v. Marshall. 1976. 424 U.S. 636.
Graves v. Barnes. 1972. 343 F. Supp. 704 (W.D. Tex.).
Graves v. Barnes. 1974. 378 F. Supp. 640 (W.D. Tex.).
Graves v. Barnes. 1976. 408 F. Supp. 1050 (W.D. Tex.).
Graves v. Barnes. 1977. 446 F. Supp. 560 (W.D. Tex.).

Gray v. Sanders. 1963. 372 U.S. 368.

Greater Houston Civic Council v. Mann. 1977. 440 F. Supp. 696 (S.D. Tex.).

Henderson v. Perry. 2005. 399 F. Supp. 2d. 756.

Kilgarlin v. Hill. 1967. 386 U.S. 120.

Kilgarlin v. Martin. 1966. 252 F. Supp. 404 (S.D. Tex.).

Kirkpatrick v. Preisler. 1969. 394 U.S. 526.

LULAC v. Perry. 2006. 548 U.S. 399.

Manley v. Texas. 2001 U.S. Dist. LEXIS 25427, *9-*10 (E.D. Tex.).

Martin v. Bush. 1964. 376 U.S. 222.

Mayfield v. Texas. 2001. (E.D. Tex.).

Mauzy v. Redistricting Board. 1971. 471 S.W. 2d 570, 573 (Tex.).

Mena v. Mosbacher. 1991. No. C-B-91-010 (U.S. Dist. Ct., S.D. Tex.).

Mena v. Richards. 1991. No. C-454-91-F (332nd Dist. Ct., Hidalgo Co.).

Moses v. City of Houston. 1973. No. H-75-1731 (S.D. Tex.).

Perez v. Texas. 2011. Civil Action No. 11-CA-360-OLG-JES-XR (Nov. 23) (U.S. Dist. Ct., W.D. Tex.).

Perry v. Del Rio. 2001. 67 S.W. 3rd (Tex.).

Perry v. Perez. Nos. 11-713, 11-714, 11-715 Supreme Court of the United States. January 20, 2012. Per curiam.

Quiroz v. Richards. 1991. No. C-4395-91-F (332nd Dist. Ct., Hidalgo Co.).

Reyes v. City of Farmers Branch. 2009. 586 F. 3d 1019 (5th Cir.).

Reynolds v. Sims. 1964. 377 U.S. 533.

Rivas v. Cuellar. 2001. Cause No. 2001-33760 (152nd Dist. Ct., Harris Co., Tex.).

Seamon v. Upham. 1982. 456 U.S. 37.

Session v. Perry. 2004. 298 F. Supp. 2d 451.

Shaw v. Reno. 1993. 509 U.S. 630.

Terrazas v. Clements. 1982. 537 F. Supp. 514.

Terrazas v. Clements. 1983. 581 F. Supp. 1319.

Terrazas v. Clements. 1984. 581 F. Supp. 1325.

Terrazas v. Ramirez. 1991. 829 S.W. 2d 712 (Tex.).

Terrazas v. Slagle. 1991. 789 F. Supp. 828 (W.D. Tex.).

Terrazas v. Slagle. 1992. 821 F. Supp. 1154, 1158 n. 4 (W.D. Tex.).

Texas v. Balderas. 2001. (E.D. Tex.).

Thornburg v. Gingles. 1986. 478 U.S. 30.

Vieth v. Jubelirer. 2004. 541 U.S. 267.

Wesberry v. Sanders. 1964. 376 U.S. 1.

Whitcomb v. Chavis. 1971. 403 U.S. 124, 141–155.

White v. Regester. 1973. 412 U.S. 755.

White v. Weiser. 1973. 412 U.S. 783.

Zimmer v. McKeithen. 1973. 485 F. 2d 1297 (5th Cir.) (en banc), aff'd sub nom. *East Carroll Parish Sch. Bd. v. Marshall.* 1976. 424 U.S. 636.

Books, Articles, and Papers Cited

Abramowitz, Alan, Brad Alexander, and Matthew Gunning. 2006. "Drawing the Line on District Competition: A Rejoinder." *PS: Political Science & Politics* 39 (1): 95–97.

Adams, William C. 1972. "Redistricting the Texas House of Representatives, 1971–1972: A Case Study in the Politics and Law of Reapportionment." MA thesis, Baylor University.

Adams, William C. 1973. "The Introduction of Single-Member House Districts in Harris, Dallas, and Bexar Counties: Some Implications for Texas Politics." Paper presented at the Southwestern Political Science Association convention, Dallas, Texas.

Aistrup, Joseph A. 1996. *The Southern Strategy Revisited: Republican Top-Down Advancement in the South.* Lexington: University Press of Kentucky.

Ansolabehere, Stephen, James M. Snyder, Jr., and Charles Stewart, III. 2000. "Old Voters, New Voters, and the Personal Vote: Using Redistricting to Measure the Incumbency Advantage." *American Journal of Political Science* 44 (1): 17–34.

Baker, Gordon E. 1966. *The Reapportionment Revolution: Representation, Political Power, and the Supreme Court.* New York: Random House.

Barone, Michael, and Grant Ujifusa. 1993. *The Almanac of American Politics 1994.* Washington, D.C.: National Journal.

Barone, Michael, Richard E. Cohen, and Grant Ujifusa. 2001. *The Almanac of American Politics 2002.* Washington, D.C.: National Journal.

Barone, Michael, Richard E. Cohen, and Grant Ujifusa. 2005. *The Almanac of American Politics 2006.* Washington, D.C.: National Journal.

Bickerstaff, Steve. 1984. "Reapportionment by State Legislatures: A Guide for the 1980s." *Southwestern Law Journal* 34: 607.

Bickerstaff, Steve. 2007. *Lines in the Sand: Congressional Redistricting in Texas and the Downfall of Tom DeLay.* Austin: University of Texas Press.

Bickerstaff, Steve. 2011. "Redistricting Texas: The History and Principles of Drawing Congressional and State Legislative Districts in Texas (1845–2010)." Austin: University of Texas School of Law.

Black, Earl, and Merle Black. 2002. *The Rise of Southern Republicans.* Cambridge, MA: Harvard University Press.

Blacksher, James, and Larry T. Menefee. 1982. "From Reynolds v. Sims to City of Mobile v. Bolden: Have the White Suburbs Commandeered the Fifteenth Amendment?" *Hastings Law Journal* 34: 1.

Boatright, Robert G. 2004. "Static Ambition in a Changing World: Legislators' Preparations for, and Responses to, Redistricting." *State Politics & Policy Quarterly* 4 (4): 436–454.

Brischetto, Robert, David R. Richards, Chandler Davidson, and Bernard

Grofman. 1994. "Texas." In Davidson, Chandler, and Bernard Grofman, eds., *Quiet Revolution in the South*. Princeton, NJ: Princeton University Press.

Buchman, Jeremy. 2003. *Drawing Lines in Quicksand: Courts, Legislatures, and Redistricting*. New York: Peter Lang Publishing.

Bullock, Charles, III, 2010. *Redistricting: The Most Political Activity in America*. Lanham, MD: Rowman & Littlefield.

Butler, Katharine Inglis. 2002. "Redistricting in a Post-Shaw Era: A Small Treatise Accompanied by Districting Guidelines for Legislators, Litigants, and Courts." *University of Richmond Law Review* 36 (1): 137–270.

Campbell, James E. 1997. "The Presidential Pulse and the 1994 Midterm Congressional Election." *Journal of Politics* 59 (3): 830–857.

Chayes, Abram. 1976. "The Role of the Judge in Public Law Litigation." *Harvard Law Review* 89: 1281–1316.

Chumlea, Wesley S. 1959. "The Politics of Legislative Apportionment in Texas 1921–1957." PhD diss. University of Texas.

Claunch, Ronald G., Wesley S. Chumlea, and James G. Dickson, Jr. 1981. "Texas." In Hardy, Leroy, Alan Heslop, and Stuart Anderson, eds., *Reapportionment Politics: The History of Redistricting in the 50 States*. Beverly Hills, CA: Sage Publications.

Cox, Adam B. and Thomas J. Miles. 2008. "Judging the Voting Rights Act." *Columbia Law Review* 108: 1–54.

Davidson, Chandler. 1972. *Biracial Politics: Conflict and Coalition in the Metropolitan South*. Baton Rouge: Louisiana University Press.

Davidson, Chandler. 1984. *Minority Vote Dilution*. Washington, D.C.: Howard University Press.

Desposato, Scott W., and John R. Petrocik. 2003. "The Variable Incumbency Advantage: New Voters, Redistricting, and the Personal Vote." *American Journal of Political Science* 47 (1): 18–32.

———. 2005. "Redistricting and Incumbency: The New Voter Effect." In Galderisi, Peter F., ed., *Redistricting in the New Millennium*. 35–63. Lanham, MD: Lexington Books.

Eckhardt, Robert C. Collection. Dolph Briscoe Center for American History of the University of Texas at Austin.

Eckhardt, Robert C. Research Files (Gary A. Keith). Dolph Briscoe Center for American History of the University of Texas at Austin.

Erikson, Robert S., and Gerald C. Wright. 2009. "Voters, Candidates, and Issues in Congressional Elections." In Dodd, Lawrence C., and Bruce I. Oppenheimer, eds., *Congress Reconsidered*. Washington, D.C.: CQ Press.

Fenno, Richard F., Jr. 1978. *Home Style: House Members in Their Districts*. Boston, MA: Little Brown.

Gaddie, Ronald Keith. 2004. "The Texas Redistricting, Measure for Measure." *Extensions*. Fall: 19. http://www.ou.edu/special/albertctr /extensions/fall2004/Gaddie.html.

Grofman, Bernard. 1990. *Voting Rights, Voting Wrongs: The Legacy of Baker v. Carr*. New York: Priority Press.

Guinier, Lani. 1994. *The Tyranny of the Majority: Fundamental Fairness in Representative Democracy*. New York: Free Press.

Hacker, Andrew. 1963. *Congressional Districting: The Issue of Equal Representation*. Washington, D.C.: Brookings Institution.

Hagard, Luther, Jr., August Spain, and Samuel Hamlett, 1965. "Legislative Redistricting in Texas." Dallas: Arnold Foundation (Southern Methodist University).

Hanson, Royce. 1966. *The Political Thicket: Reapportionment and Constitutional Democracy*. Englewood Cliffs, NJ: Prentice-Hall.

Harris County Democratic Party Collection, Dolph Briscoe Center for American History of the University of Texas at Austin.

Hayes, Danny, and Seth C. McKee. 2009. "The Participatory Effects of Redistricting." *American Journal of Political Science* 53 (4): 1006–1023.

Hebert, J. Gerald, Paul M. Smith, Martina E. Vandenberg, and Michael B. DeSanctis. 2010. *The Realist's Guide to Redistricting: Avoiding the Legal Pitfalls*. 2nd ed. Chicago: American Bar Association.

Herskowitz, Mickey. 1994. *Sharpstown Revisited: Frank Sharp and a Tale of Dirty Politics in Texas*. Austin: Eakin Press.

Hetherington, Marc J., Bruce A. Larson, and Suzanne Globbeti. 2003. "The Redistricting Cycle and Strategic Candidate Decisions in U.S. House Races." *Journal of Politics* 65 (4): 1221–1235.

Hill, Kevin A., and Nicole C. Rae. 2000. "What Happened to the Democrats in the South? US House Elections, 1992–1996." *Party Politics* 6 (1): 5–22.

Hood, M. V., III, and Seth C. McKee. 2010. "Stranger Danger: Redistricting, Incumbent Recognition, and Vote Choice." *Social Science Quarterly* 91 (2): 344–358.

House Journal. 1965. 59th Texas Legislature, vol. 1, January 27.

House Research Organization. 1992. "Redistricting for the Nineties: A Progress Report." Special Legislative Report No. 175.

Institute of Public Affairs. 1966. *The Fifty-Ninth Texas Legislature: A Review of its Work*. Austin: University of Texas.

Jacobson, Gary C. 1990. *The Electoral Origins of Divided Government: Competition in U.S. House Elections, 1946–1988*. Boulder, CO: Westview Press.

———. 2000. "Reversal of Fortune: The Transformation of U.S. House Elections in the 1990s." In Brady, David W., John F. Cogan, and Morris P. Fiorina, eds., *Continuity and Change in House Elections*. Stanford, CA: Stanford University Press.

———. 2009. *The Politics of Congressional Elections*. New York: Pearson Longman.

Jensen, James R. 1964. "Legislative Apportionment in Texas." University of Houston Social Studies Vol. 2, Public Affairs Research Center.

Keith, Gary A. 2007. *Eckhardt: There Once was a Congressman from Texas*. Austin: University of Texas Press.

Key, V. O., Jr. 1949. *Southern Politics in State and Nation*. New York: Vintage Books.

Kinch, Sam, Jr., and Ben Procter. 1972. *Texas under a Cloud*. Austin: Jenkins.

Kousser, J. Morgan. 1974. *The Shaping of Southern Politics: Suffrage Restriction and the Establishment of the One-Party South, 1880–1910*. New Haven: Yale University Press.

Lawson, Steven F. 1985. *In Pursuit of Power: Southern Blacks and Electoral Politics, 1965–1982*. New York: Columbia University Press.

Levinson, Sanford. 2002. "Symposium: Baker v. Carr: A Commemorative Symposium: Panel II: One Person, One Vote: A Theoretical and Practical Examination: One Person, One Vote: A Mantra in Need of Meaning." *North Carolina Law Review*, 80 (May): 1269–1297.

Lipsitz, George. 2011. *How Racism Takes Place*. Philadelphia: Temple University Press.

Lynch, Timothy. 2011. "Drawn to (not) Run: District Continuity and Quality Challengers." Paper presented at the annual meeting of the Southern Political Science Association. New Orleans, LA.

McKay, Robert B. 1965. *Reapportionment: The Law and Politics of Equal Representation*. New York: Twentieth Century Fund.

McKee, Seth C. 2010. *Republican Ascendancy in Southern U.S. House Elections*. Boulder, CO: Westview Press.

———. 2008a. "The Effects of Redistricting on Voting Behavior in Incumbent U.S. House Elections, 1992–1994." *Political Research Quarterly* 61 (1): 122–133.

———. 2008b. "Redistricting and Familiarity with U.S. House Candidates." *American Politics Research* 36 (6): 962–979.

McKee, Seth C., and Brian K. Arbour. 2006. "Cracking Back: The Effectiveness of Partisan Redistricting in the Texas House of Representatives." *American Review of Politics* 26 (Winter): 385–403.

McKee, Seth C., Jeremy M. Teigen, and Mathieu Turgeon. 2006. "The Partisan Impact of Congressional Redistricting: The Case of Texas, 2001–2003." *Social Science Quarterly* 87 (2): 308–317.

McKee, Seth C., and Daron K. Shaw. 2005. "Redistricting in Texas: Institutionalizing Republican Ascendancy." In Galderisis, Peter F., ed., *Redistricting in the New Millennium*. Lanham, MD: Lexington Books.

McKenzie, Mark J. 2012. "The Influence of Partisanship, Ideology, and the Law on Redistricting Decisions in the Federal Courts." *Political Research Quarterly* 65 (4): 799–813.

Montejano, David. 1987. *Anglos and Mexican Americans in the Making of Texas, 1836–1986.* Austin: University of Texas Press.

Mosbacher, Robert A., Sr. 2010. *Going to Windward, A Mosbacher Family Memoir.* College Station: Texas A&M Press.

National Conference of State Legislatures. 2009. "Redistricting Law 2010." Washington, D.C.: National Conference of State Legislatures.

Perales, Nina, Luis Figueroa, and Criselda G. Rivas. 2008. "Voting Rights in Texas: 1982–2006." *Review of Law and Social Justice* 17 (2): 713–759.

Persily, Nathaniel. 2005. "Forty Years in the Political Thicket: Judicial Review of the Redistricting Process Since Reynolds v. Sims." In Mann, Thomas E., and Bruce E. Cain, eds., *Party Lines: Competition, Partisanship, and Congressional Redistricting.* Washington, D.C.: Brookings Institution.

Petrocik, John R., and Scott W. Desposato. 1998. "The Partisan Consequences of Majority-Minority Redistricting in the South, 1992 and 1994." *Journal of Politics* 60 (3): 613–633.

———. 2004. "Incumbency and Short-Term Influences on Voters." *Political Research Quarterly* 57 (3): 363–373.

Richards, David R. 2002. *Once Upon a Time in Texas: A Liberal in the Lone Star State.* Austin: Focus on American History Series, Center for American History, University of Texas Press. 2002.

Rossiter, Clinton, ed. 1961. "James Madison's Federalist No. 57." *The Federalist Papers.* New York: New American Library.

Rush, Mark E. 2000. "Redistricting and Partisan Fluidity: Do We Really Know a Gerrymander When We See One?" *Political Geography* 19: 249–260.

Scammon, Richard. 1966. *America Votes.* Washington, D.C.: Congressional Quarterly Weekly.

Schattschneider, E. E. 1960. *The Semisovereign People: A Realist's View of Democracy in America.* New York: Holt, Rinehart and Winston.

Simon, Dennis. 2002. "Texans in the United States House of Representatives: A History of Electoral, Partisan, and Ideological Change, 1936–2000." Presented at Jim Wright Symposium on Texas Congressional Leaders, Texas Christian University, Fort Worth, Texas.

Southwestern Reporter. 1982. No. 97–417.

Stephens, Jerry D. 1966. "A Case Study of Legislative Reapportionment in Texas 1961–1966." MA thesis, University of Texas.

Stokes, Donald. 1998. "Is There a Better Way to Redistrict?" In Grofman, Bernard, ed., *Race and Redistricting in the 1990s.* New York: Agathon Press.

Stonecash, Jeffrey M. 2008. *Reassessing the Incumbency Effect*. New York: Cambridge University Press.

Texas Legislative Council. 1964. "Congressional Redistricting." Report No. 58-2.

Texas Legislative Council. 2010. "Overview of Texas Redistricting." http://www.tlc.state.tx.us/redist/history_overview_congress.html. Accessed September 19, 2010.

Texas State Directory. 1994. Austin: Texas State Directory Press.

Watson, Dwight David. 1995 (March). "From Smoke to Fire: Causes of the 1967 Texas Southern University Riot." Paper presented at Texas State Historical Association, San Antonio.

Winburn, Jonathan. 2008. *The Realities of Redistricting: Following the Rules and Limiting Gerrymandering in State Legislative Redistricting*. Lanham, MD: Lexington Books.

Yoshinaka, Antoine, and Chad Murphy. 2009. "Partisan Gerrymandering and Population Instability: Completing the Redistricting Puzzle." *Political Geography* 28 (8): 451–462.

Zelden, Charles L. 2002. *Voting Rights on Trial: A Handbook with Cases, Laws, and Documents*. Santa Barbara, CA: ABC-CLIO.

Periodicals and Websites Cited

Austin American-Statesman
    8 October 1994. John Knaggs. "Night Hawk served up good food, memories."
CBS Reports
    26 August 1981. "Best Little Statehouse in Texas."
Dallas Morning News
    25 February 1931.
    21 March 1931.
House Study Group Daily Floor Report
    27 May 1981. "HB 960 Bill Analysis."
Houston Chronicle
    20 October 1963.
    23 October 1963. "Solons Denounce Connally's Stand on Redistricting."
    16 June 1964, 15. Tutt, Bob. "State Reapportionment to be Pushed in Texas."
    12 January 1965, 21. "Harris Legislators Show Mixed Reaction to Districting Proposal."
    26 January 1965.
    7 April 1965. "Rep. Floyd Unhappy with Plan Dividing Harris into Five Districts."

6 May 1965. "House Stamps OK on Districting Proposal."

30 May 1965.

31 May 1965. "Redistricting Errors Face Legislators."

23 October 1971.

Houston Post

1 June 1965, 4. "26 in House Sign Protest over Congressional Redistricting."

6 June 1971.

23 January 1972.

Houston Tribune

18 February 1965, 1. "Redistricting issue brings odd alliance: Eckhardt, GOP favor same plan."

Liberal Arts Instructional Technology Services of the University of Texas

"The Partisan Composition of the Texas Legislature," http://www.laits.utexas.edu/txp_media/html/leg/features/0303_01/slide1.html and http://www.laits.utexas.edu/txp_media/html/leg/features/0303_01/slide2.html.

MALDEF

http://maldef.org/voting_rights/litigation/index.html

http://maldef.org/redistricting/index.html

New York Times

26 August 1981. Molly Ivins, "TV: 'CBS Reports' Views Texas Legislature."

Texas Legislative Council

"1990s Redistricting," http://www.tlc.state.tx.us/redist/history_1990.html.

"1990s Redistricting Chronology," http://www.tlc.state.tx.us/redist/chron_1990.htm.

Texas Observer

11 June 1965, 8.

TSU Herald

31 August 2007. "Bricks without Straw—The almost forgotten 40 year history of the Tigerwalk."

Think Progress

Millhiser, Ian. "Rep. Paul Broun Tries To Defund Voting Rights Act." http://thinkprogress.org/justice/2012/05/10/482210/rep-paul-broun-tries-to-defund-voting-rights-act/

U.S. Code Congressional and Administrative News

1982

About the Contributors

José Garza is a solo practitioner in San Antonio, Texas. He received his BA from Texas A&I University, his MA from the University of Texas at San Antonio (UTSA), and his JD from St. Mary's School of Law (in San Antonio). He has extensive litigation experience in the public and private sector, specializing in redistricting, federal voting rights, and civil rights cases. In addition to working with the League of United Latin American Citizens (LULAC), he spent ten years with the Mexican American Legal Defense and Educational Fund (MALDEF) and almost twenty years with Texas Rural/RioGrande Legal Aid (TRLA). He has argued election law issues before U.S. district courts, courts of appeal, and the U.S. Supreme Court, as well as state courts. Garza has also taught at St. Mary's School of Law and the University of Texas School of Law. Most recently, he worked as counsel to the Mexican American Legislative Caucus of the Texas House of Representatives, analyzing and litigating redistricting issues, including giving the oral arguments to the U.S. Supreme Court in the case of *Perry v. Perez et al.*

Gary A. Keith received his BA from Baylor University and his PhD in politics from Brandeis University. He worked at the Texas legislature from the 1970s to the 1990s. He has taught at numerous colleges and universities and is currently pre-law advisor and Associate Professor of Government and International Affairs at the University of the Incarnate Word (in San Antonio). Keith is the author of *Eckhardt: There Once was a Congressman from Texas* and lead author of *Texas Politics and Government*.

Seth C. McKee got his BS in political science and MS in economics from Oklahoma State University and his PhD in Government from the University of Texas. He is currently Associate Professor of Political Science at the University of South Florida St. Petersburg. McKee is an American politics scholar whose areas of research and teaching include American institutions, political behavior, southern politics, political parties, and redistricting. He has published "Cracking Back: The Effectiveness of Partisan Redistricting in the Texas House of Representatives," with Brian K. Arbour, in *American Review of Politics*; "The Partisan Impact of Congressional Redistricting: The Case of Texas, 2001–2003," with Jeremy M. Teigen and Mathieu Turgeon, in *Social Science Quarterly*; and "Redistricting in Texas: Institutionalizing Republican Ascendancy," with Daron R. Shaw, in *Redistricting in the New Millennium*.

Mark J. McKenzie received his BA in government from the University of Texas at Austin and his JD from the University of Texas School of Law. After practicing general litigation for three years, he earned his PhD in government from the University of Texas in 2007. He is currently Assistant Professor of Political Science at Texas Tech University. McKenzie's research focuses on redistricting and the courts, judicial politics, elections, political behavior, and the Electoral College. He has published articles in *Judicature*, *Justice System Journal*, *American Politics Research*, and *Politics & Policy*.

J. D. Pauerstein got his BA from the University of Texas at Austin and his JD from Baylor University School of Law, where he was editor-in-chief of the *Baylor Law Review*. He is a partner in the San Antonio firm Rosenthal Pauerstein Sandoloski

Agather LLP, where he heads the Disputes and Litigation section. Mr. Pauerstein has represented elected officials in connection with campaign finance reporting and related issues, and has represented parties to election contests and recounts, Voting Rights Act litigation, and federal and state redistricting litigation.

David R. Richards got his BA from Baylor University and his JD from the University of Texas. He moved to Dallas, where he practiced labor law. Returning to Austin in 1969, Richards practiced labor and civil rights law, then served as head of litigation for the Texas Attorney General in the 1980s. He has served as counsel in redistricting lawsuits from the 1970s to the present—both for plaintiff groups and for the state. Richards is author of *Once Upon a Time in Texas: A Liberal in the Lone Star State*.

Craig A. Washington got his BA from Prairie View A&M University, then earned his JD from Texas Southern University School of Law (now named the Thurgood Marshall School of Law), where he graduated first in his class. He won election to the Texas House of Representatives, where he served (D-Houston) from 1973 to 1982. He was named Speaker Pro Tem in his last House term. Washington was elected to the state Senate in 1982, where he served until 1989. *Texas Monthly* named him one of the Ten Best Legislators on three occasions. In 1989 he won a special election to Congress, where he served through 1994. Thus, Washington served as a state legislator and as a congressman during redistricting sessions from the 1970s to the 1990s. He has taught law at Thurgood Marshall School of Law and currently practices with the Washington Law Firm in Houston.

Index